MW00465063

Table of Contents

What Dave's Clients Say

"I am pleased to recommend Dave Kauppi and MidMarket Capital. Our transaction was recently concluded and the outcome has completely met our expectations. I believe that MidMarket Capital found the best buyer for our company and facilitated realization of the best value the market had to offer."

Jim Leineweber, President,
The Systems House, Des Plaines IL

"I want to thank you for your efforts in the sale of our business. Our attorney originally recommended you because he knew of your experience in selling smaller technology companies. In retrospect, I now appreciate how important that was in us achieving our desired outcome. Thanks again."

Rod Hart President,
Advantage Health dba Flexistaff

"MMC understood our business and our market while presenting us to hundreds of qualified buyers. We are happy that we have completed the transaction with the best partner for our future. We were impressed with your experience in the deal making process, deal structure, and the negotiating process. Of particular importance to us was your commitment and passion to fight for our transaction value. I very much appreciated your strong ethics, and fighting for my best interests through the entire process."

Mike Sherwood, President, Base36

"As I reflect on this process, I am glad that we had MidMarket Capital as our advocate in representing Small Business Computers of New England to the market. I really appreciated that you understood and defended our commitment to both our employees and our clients to the companies that made proposals. MMC pursued hundreds of industry and strategic buyers and we feel that the transaction was completed with the best buyer."

Gene Calvano, President,
Small Business Computers of New England, Inc.

"I am very happy with the outcome and feel that our company and our team have been matched with the company that is the best fit. Your process exposed us to hundreds of healthcare information technology buyers and resulted in the best terms and price for our sale."

Jerry Iverson, President,
Healthcare Decision Systems, Inc

"When we decided to seek an acquisition, we knew that we would need some help. We had no idea how grueling and complex the process would be. We are very appreciative that MMC was our partner in this journey.

We would highly recommend MidMarket Capital Advisors to represent software and information technology owners that are seeking to sell their company."

Neil Morgan, President, BrightStar Partners, Inc

"Since MMC led the negotiations, we were able to preserve a great working relationship with the buyer. Most importantly, your leadership in the overall acquisition process allowed the VSA team to focus on our Clients and not the hour-to-hour gyrations of the deal. Your team was always straight and direct which is very important to me. Lastly, you earned my implicit trust and confidence. I never doubted that my "safety net" was always in place and our best interests were top priority.

This project was not simply selling a company. For us, you crafted our futures and we couldn't be happier with the results!!!"

Ann Van Slyck, RN, MSN, CNAA, FAAN,
Chief Executive Officer. Van Slyck & Associates

Selling
Your
Software
Company

How the Merger
and Acquisition
Process *Really*
Works and what you
can do to win!

About the Author

Dave Kauppi is the editor of The Exit Strategist Newsletter, rated by New York Times Small Business as best M&A newsletter for deal terms and strategy. He is an active Blogger at http://sellsoftwarecompany.blogspot.com/ Dave's articles have been published in Family Business Magazine, Crain's Chicago Business, Directors and Boards, Divestopedia, and many others.

Dave is a Merger and Acquisition Advisor and President with MidMarket Capital, Inc. MMC is a private investment banking, merger & acquisition firm specializing in providing corporate finance and

:es to entrepreneurs and middle

lients in information technology,

1, and a variety of industries.

; Merger and Acquisition practice after a twenty-year career within the information technology industry. His varied background includes positions in hardware sales, IT Services (IBM's Service Bureau Corp. and Comdisco Disaster Recovery), Software Sales, computer leasing, datacom, and Internet. The firm counsels clients in the areas of merger and acquisition and divestitures, achieving strategic value, deal structure and terms, competitive negotiations, and "smart equity" capital raises. Dave is a Certified Business Intermediary (CBI), is a registered financial services advisor representative and securities agent with a Series 63 license. Dave graduated with a degree in finance from the Wharton School of Business, University of Pennsylvania. For more information or a free consultation please contact Dave Kauppi at (630) 325-0123, email davekauppi@midmarkcap.com or visit our web page http://www.midmarkcap.com/mmc

Acknowledgements

I would like to thank my many customers over the years that have joined me in the trenches to fight the good fight in achieving strategic value. Thanks to my dad, Donald Kauppi for instilling in me my love for coaching and teaching, my mom, Helen, whose sense of humor is my source of remaining cool under fire. Thanks to my sweet and beautiful wife, Paula, who greets me and each day with a smile. Finally, I want to thank my kids Brian, Steven, and Jenna who bring me back to center and help me understand what is really important.

Introduction

This book took me seventeen years to write. Well, not literally. What I really should say is that over seventeen years in representing sellers of technology companies, we have gained the experiences that comprise this manuscript. It is different from an individual business seller telling their story because theirs is limited to one deal. Our experience is from representing a broad cross section of technology businesses to a wide range of buyers.

No two deals are the same and we continue to learn with each new engagement. Often times the lessons learned in the business sale process are very expensive lessons for business owners that try to navigate this process alone. What we do is not rocket science or brain surgery, but it is dependent on building on a strong base of experiences. Maybe an example will help illustrate. Remember the first time you did a project from changing your car oil to mounting a new door? I do. When I mounted my first door it took me over 4 hours and a number of corrections and adjustments. My second door took me one third the amount of time with very few errors. Now think about that first time experience with a far more complex process with millions of dollars at stake.

This book consists of many articles and blog posts we have written over the years. Our purpose is to capture the valuable lessons from our engagements and then share them with potential clients while they are still fresh in our minds. The more important function that this content performs is to prepare current clients of MidMarket Capital, Inc. for each stage of the merger and acquisition process before we enter it. We send them the article on buyer questions, or letters of intent, or corporate visits, or buyer negotiation tactics in a stress free teaching environment. We make sure that they are prepared prior to the often times very emotional stage of the deal process. If a deal blows up because our client was unprepared, it is on us. So our sellers are prepared.

I like to compare excellence in M&A transactions to excellence in golf. In golf you have to be at the top in every aspect of the game in order to excel. You can't just be a great driver or great putter and expect to win. You have to be a good ball striker, scrambler, chipper, putter, driver, sand player and thinker to reach the top of the game. It is the same in M&A. It does your client no good to create huge value with a great business marketing campaign only to give it away with a loosely worded letter of intent and the buyer hacking away at the value through due diligence and closing.

The successful M&A process is multi-faceted and each stage must be performed at the highest level in order to achieve maximum strategic value for the client. As we tell our clients, if you want to sell for strategic value you must first create a great technology and great company. You must then be able to capture and articulate that value in a professionally managed and competitive M&A process. That process consists of being able to convince qualified buyers the strategic value of your company in their hands. Several like-minded buyers should be engaged in a competitive bidding process which must be artfully done because buyers withdraw if they think you are overtly playing one against the other. That part, to use our golf analogy, is just the "drive for show". The "putt for dough" part is to intelligently craft and negotiate a Letter of Intent that prevents erosion in transaction value through due diligence, the definitive purchase agreement and closing. We hope you enjoy and learn from THE INSIDER'S GUIDE TO ACHIEVING STRATEGIC VALUE.

Please feel welcome to join our free Exit Strategist Newsletter rated by New York Times Small Business as "Best for deal terms and strategy" by visiting http://midmarkcap.com/mmc/seller-resources/ and also receive our widely downloaded guide ESSENTIAL READING FOR TECH COMPANY ENTREPRENEURS 20 BOOKS THAT WILL CHANGE HOW YOU LOOK AT YOUR BUSINESS

CHAPTER 1

Valuation

1.1 – CREATIVE APPROACHES TO DRIVING VALUE DURING THE M&A PROCESS

One of the most challenging aspects of selling an information technology company is coming up with a business valuation. Sometimes the valuations provided by the market (translation – a completed transaction) defy all logic. In other industry segments there are some pretty handy rules of thumb for valuation metrics. In one industry it may be 1 X Revenue, in another it could be 4.5 X EBITDA.

Since it is critical to our business to help our information technology clients maximize their

business selling price, I have given
thought. Why are some of these
valuations so high? It is because of the pro...
leverage of technology. A simple example is what is
Microsoft's incremental cost to produce the next
copy of Office Professional? Actually, it should be
close to $0 because most copies are downloaded.
Let's say the license cost is $400. The gross margin
is north of 99%. That does not happen in manufacturing or services or retail or most other industries.

One problem in selling a small technology company is that they do not have any of the brand name,
distribution, or standards leverage that the big companies possess. So, on their own, they cannot create
this profitability leverage. The acquiring company,
however, does not want to compensate the small
seller for the post acquisition results that are directly attributable to the buyer's market presence. This
is what we refer to as the valuation gap.

What we attempt to do is to help the buyer justify paying a much higher price than a pre-acquisi-
tion financial valuation of the target company. In
other words, we want to get strategic value for our
seller. Below are the factors that we use in our
analysis:

1. Cost for the buyer to write the code internally – Many years ago, Barry Boehm, in his book, Software Engineering Economics, developed a constructive cost model for projecting the programming costs for writing computer code. He called it the COCOMO model. It was quite detailed and complex, but I have boiled it down and simplified it for our purposes. We have the advantage of estimating the "projects" retrospectively because we already know the number of lines of code comprising our client's products. In general terms he projected that it takes 3.6 person months to write one thousand SLOC (source lines of code). So if you looked at a senior software engineer at a $70,000 fully loaded compensation package writing a program with 15,000 SLOC, your calculation is as follows – 15 X 3.6 = 54 person months X $5,800 per month = $313,200 divided by 15,000 = $20.88/SLOC.

Before you guys with 1,000,000 million lines of code get too excited about your $20.88 million business value, there are several caveats. Unfortunately the market does not care and will not pay for what it cost you to develop your product. Secondly, this information is designed to help us understand what it might cost the buyer to develop it internally so that he starts his own build versus buy analysis. Thirdly, we have to apply discounts to this analysis if the software is three generations old legacy code, for example. In that case, it is discounted by 90%. You are no longer a technology sale with high profitability leverage. They are essentially acquiring your customer base and the valuation will not be that exciting.

If, however, your application is a brand new application that has legs, start sizing your yacht. Examples of this might be a messaging application, mobile payments, file sharing, or social media. The second high value platform would be where your software technology "leap frogs" a popular legacy application. An example of this is when we sold a company that had completely rewritten their legacy distribution management platform for a new vertical market in Microsoft .Net. They leap frogged the dominant player in that space that was supporting multiple green screen solutions. Our client became a compelling strategic acquisition. Fast forward one year and I hear the acquirer is selling one of these $100,000 systems per week. Now that's leverage!

2. Most acquirers could write the code them-

selves, but we suggest they analyze the cost of their time to market delay. Believe me, with first mover advantage from a competitor or, worse, customer defections, there is a very real cost of not having your product today. We were able to convince one buyer that they would be able to justify our seller's entire purchase price based on the number of client defections their acquisition would prevent. As it turned out, the buyer had a huge install base and through multiple prior acquisitions was maintaining six disparate software platforms to deliver essentially the same functionality.

This was very expensive to maintain and they passed those costs on to their disgruntled install base. The buyer had been promising upgrades for a few years, but nothing was delivered. Customers were beginning to sign on with their major competitor. Our pitch to the buyer was to make this acquisition, demonstrate to your client base that you are really providing an upgrade path and give notice of support withdrawal for 4 or 5 of the other platforms. The acquisition was completed and, even though their customers that were contemplating leaving did not immediately upgrade, they did not defect either. Apparently the devil that you know is better than the devil you don't in the world of information technology.

3. Another arrow in our valuation driving quiver for our sellers is we restate historical financials using the pricing power of the brand name acquirer. We had one client that was a small IT company that had developed a fine piece of software that compared favorably with a large, publicly traded company's solution. Our product had the same functionality, ease of use, and open systems platform, but there was one very important difference. The end-user customer's perception of risk was far greater with the little IT company that could be "out of business tomorrow." We were literally able to double the financial performance of our client on paper and present a compelling argument to the big company buyer that those economics would be immediately available to him post acquisition. It certainly was not GAP Accounting, but it was effective as a tool to drive transaction value.

4. Financials are important so we have to acknowledge this aspect of buyer valuation as well. We generally like to build in a baseline value (before we start adding the strategic value components) of 2 X contractually recurring revenue during the cur-

rent year. So, for example, if the company has monthly maintenance contracts of $100,000 times 12 months = $1.2 million X 2 = $2.4 million as a baseline company value component. Another component we add is for any contracts that extend beyond one year. We take an estimate of the gross margin produced in the firm contract years beyond year one and assign a 5 X multiple to that and discount it to present value.

Let's use an example where they had 4 years remaining on a services contract and the last 3 years were $200,000 per year in revenue with approximately 50% gross margin. We would take the final three years of $100,000 annual gross margin and present value it at a 5% discount rate resulting in $265,616. This would be added to the earlier 2 X recurring year 1 revenue from above. Again, this financial analysis is to establish a baseline, before we pile on the strategic value components.

5. We try to assign values for miscellaneous assets that the seller is providing to the buyer. Don't overlook the strategic value of Blue Chip Accounts. Those accounts become a platform for the buyer's entire product suite being sold post acquisition into an "installed account." It is far easier to sell add-on

applications and products into an existing account than it is to open up that new account. These strategic accounts can have huge value to a buyer.

6. Another approach we use is a customer acquisition cost model to drive value in the eyes of a potential buyer. Let's say that your sales person at 100% of Quota earns total salary and commissions of $125,000 and sells 5 net new accounts. That would mean that your base customer acquisition cost per account was $25,000. Add a 20% company overhead for the 85 accounts, for example, and the company value, using this methodology would be $2,550,000.

7. Our final valuation component is what we call the defensive factor. This is very real in the information technology arena. What is the value to a large firm of preventing his competitor from acquiring your technology and improving their competitive position in the marketplace. One of our clients had an healthcare outcomes database and nurse staffing software algorithm. The owner was the recognized expert in this area and had industry credibility. This was a small add on application to two large industry players' integrated hospital applications suite. This module was viewed as providing a

slight features advantage to the company that could integrate it with their main systems. The selling price for one of these major software systems to a hospital chain was often more than $50 million. The value paid for our client was determined, not by the financial performance of our client, but by the competitive edge they could provide post acquisition. Our client did very well on her company sale.

After reading this you may be saying to yourself, come on, this is a little far-fetched. These components do have real value, but that value is open to a broad interpretation by the marketplace. We are attempting to assign metrics to a very subjective set of components. The buyers are smart, and experienced in the M&A process and quite frankly, they try to deflect these artistic approaches to driving up their financial outlay. The best leverage point we have is that those buyers know that we are presenting the same analysis to their competitors and they don't know which component or components of value that we have presented will resonate with their competition. In the final analysis, we are just trying to provide the buyers some reasonable explanation for their board of directors to justify paying 8 X revenues for an acquisition.

1.2 – STRATEGIC VALUE IS NOT AUTOMATIC

Wow did I get a real world demonstration of the saying, "Beauty is in the eyes of the beholder." If I could rephrase that to the business sale situation it could be, Strategic Value is in the eyes of each unique buyer." We were representing a small company that had an online hospital information system, specifically a nurse staffing and shift bidding and scheduling application. They had gotten a handful of sales from some of the early adapters in the hospital space.

The owner was at a cross-roads. To keep up with their very well funded competitor (some of the Web MD investors launched a competing product) they recognized that they would require a substantial capital investment. They understood that they had a window of opportunity to achieve a meaningful footprint before their much better capitalized competitor established market dominance. They realized that their ability to scale was critical to their ultimate success and felt their best route was to sell out to a strategic buyer.

The good news is that the owner made a very sound decision going this route rather than trying to raise capital. Speed to market was critical and he reasoned that the strategic acquirer route would be more expeditious than the capital raise approach. He recognized that his company, standing alone would not be able to overcome the conservative hospital decision process of going with the well-known, branded larger vendor.

The ideal company buyer is a larger company that provides information technology and software products in the human resources and staffing departments within hospitals. They could plug this software capability into their existing product line and distribution channel and immediately drive additional sales. They would strengthen their position within their accounts and prospects by offering an additional productivity enhancing product that would promote companion product sales. It would also provide a unique door opener to other major accounts that would want this high ROI product.

With the input from our clients we located a handful of companies that fit this profile. We were pretty excited at the prospects of our potential buyers recognizing all of these value drivers and making purchase offers that were not based on historical financial performance. The book, memorandum, confidential business review, executive summary, or whatever your investment banker or merger and acquisition advisor calls it, will certainly point out all of the strategic value that this company can provide the company that is lucky enough to buy it.

As part of the buying process we usually distribute the book and then get a round of additional questions from the buyer. We submit those to our client and then provide the answers to the buyer with a request for a conference call. We had moved the process to this point with two buyers that we thought were similar strategic buyers. The two conference calls were surprisingly totally different.

The first one included the Merger and Acquisition guy and the Chief Financial Officer. Their questions really indicated that they were used to analyzing potential acquisitions strictly from a financial perspective. They focused on our client's EBITDA, gross margin, growth rate, cost of customer acquisition and other historical financial metrics. We had a very bad vibe from these guys. They were refusing to recognize that this was a high gross margin product growing in sales by over 200% year over year and had a higher level of selling and promotional expense than a mature commodity software application. We couldn't determine if they just didn't get it or were they being dumb like a fox to dampen our value expectations.

The second call from the other company included the Merger and Acquisition guy and the HR systems product manager. The whole tone of the questioning was different. The questions focused on growth in sales, pricing power, new client potential, growth strategy, their status at the major accounts, and ownership of intellectual property.

Well we got the initial offers and they could not have been more different. The first company could not get beyond evaluating the acquisition as if it were moving forward in the hands of the current owner and with his ability to grow the business. Their offer was an EBITDA multiple bid without taking into consideration that the product sales had grown at over 200% year over year and the marketing and promotional expenses were heavily front end loaded. In spite of our efforts to convey that this was a competitive bid situation and we were in front of their competitors, they refused to be moved off this financial approach to the valuation of this high-potential product.

The second company understood the strategic

value and they reflected it in the offer. We had done a good deal of strategic positioning with this buyer. We discussed with them the tremendous potential growth rate they could achieve with this product being incorporated into their product portfolio and being sold into their install base and prospects through their highly developed distribution channels. We recognized that they would not pay for this potential with all cash at closing. So we encouraged them to include a significant portion of transaction value in an earnout based on product sales over the next three years.

The financial buyer's first offer was all cash at close. When we compared that offer to the conservative mid-point of our strategic buyer's combined cash and earn out offer, our transaction value was 300% higher with the strategic buyer. This was the biggest disparity between offers I have ever experienced, but it was quite instructive as to the necessity to get multiple opinions by the market of potential buyers. This is especially important where a meaningful percentage of the company's value is contained in their technology and intellectual property.

There are some companies that no matter how hard we try will not be perceived as a strategic acquisition by any buyer and they are going to sell at a financial multiple. Those companies are often main street type companies like gas stations, convenience stores and dry cleaners that are acquired by individual buyers. If you are a B2B company, software, high tech, healthcare technology company, have a competitive niche, and are not selling into a commodity type pricing structure, it is important to get multiple buyers involved and to get at least one of those buyers to acknowledge the strategic value.

1.3 – THE MARKET PROVIDES MANY OPINIONS ON THE VALUE OF A TECH BUSINESS

We are deep into the sell-side process for one of our clients. We have received several competing bids from industry buyers, private equity groups, and private equity groups with platform companies similar to our client. To assist our clients in evaluating the proposed transaction we compile in an Excel spreadsheet our deal comparison worksheet. We capture various components of the deal and enter it into a column for each buyer. Variables we highlight are purchase price, cash at closing, seller note amount and interest rate, earnout, owner's transition salary, and any other component of value identified in the respective letters of intent.

With this fresh on my mind, I receive a call from an entrepreneur who has developed a transformative technology and has had some initial sales wins in B2B and B2Government. He has hit the wall of sales growth on his own because his technology is such that it will be used in large business and governmental applications. Those buyers want to deal with large companies.

One of the companies that has a companion product to his (in a client installation both products will be used together) has expressed an interest in buying this company. The owner's impression, without any specific information on value from the potential buyer is they will offer a number that would be a 40 X multiple of current revenue - off the charts, but not unusual for me to hear from similar prior tech entrepreneurs' inquiries.

So after some exchange of data and a couple of conversations, I try to pin this guy down on what he would like me to do for him. He says he wants me to help him negotiate a deal for him with this one buyer. Well of course, I go into my Pavlovian response of "the only way to determine the true value of your technology is through a professionally directed full M&A engagement where you invite qualified buyers into a soft auction process."

Well he is not buying my point and keeps moving me back to a limited engagement where I would help drive maximum value from this one buyer. I was trying to find a better way to communicate my message and I decided to draw on my deal comparison worksheet from above. I told him that this client was a pretty well defined company, steady predictable revenues, a modest growth rate, stable profit margins, and no proprietary technology. In other words it would be very easy to value this company. It would be 3.9 X EBITDA, 70% cash at close and a seller note for 30% all day long.

So I am explaining to him that with highly qualified and sophisticated buyers, I expected the variance in the bids to be 10-15%, maximum. Well, was I ever wrong and was I ever surprised about the magnitude of difference from low bids to high bids. The spread was over 40%. We had hundreds of buyers when we started, 50 NDA's executed and 13 LOI's. I can tell my client with confidence that we know the value of his business and he feels confident he is not leaving money on the table.

I explained to my potential new client that the

process he was trying to convince me to launch on his behalf would not be one that I could have confidence that I was providing the highest and best price his technology could warrant. It is even more variable for these tech companies who have potentially exponential technology. The opinions of value are even more dramatic and the differences between top and bottom could be Millions of dollars. Which one is this single buyer, the top, the bottom, or somewhere in between.? Even the smartest venture capitalists guess wrong more than 80% of the time.

Why would you agree to a process that tries to shortcut this proven market value discovery process? The best case is that every time you hear about the latest Unicorn $ Billion start up, you wonder if that could be me. The worst case is that you actually left $ millions on the table because of a flawed exit process.

1.4 – VALUING THE GROWTH RATE IN THE SALE OF A TECHNOLOGY COMPANY

In the sale of privately held businesses there seems to be no mechanism and certainly no attempt on the part of buyers to account for the selling company's growth rate. In the public market this factor is widely recognized and is accounted for with an improvement on the PE multiple, the PEG or Price Earnings Growth multiple. Because there is no exact translation between EBITDA multiple (the primary valuation metric for privately held companies) and Earnings Per Share and PE multiple (the primary valuation metric for publicly traded stocks), the purpose of this article is to try to calculate an adjustment factor that can be applied against the EBITDA valuation metric in order to present a more accurate accounting for differences in growth rate for the valuation of privately held companies.

Experienced business buyers are masters of setting the rules for how they calculate the value of a business they are attempting to acquire. You may think that a 5 X multiple of EBITDA or 1 X Sales would be pretty cut and dried, but in practice it is open for creative interpretation. For example, if you just had your best year ever and your EBITDA was $2 million and the market valuation was 5 X, then you would expect a $10 million offer. Not so fast. The buyer may counter with, "That last year was an anomaly and we should normalize EBITDA performance as an average of the last three years." That average turns out to be $1.5 million and like magic your purchase offer evaporates to $7.5 million. On the flip side, if you just had your worst year at $1 million EBITDA, you can bet the buyer will use that as your metric for value.

The three owners paid themselves $100,000 each in salary, but the buyer asserts that the fair market value salary for a replacement for each senior manager is really $150,000. They apply this total $150,000 EBITDA adjustment and your valuation drops by another $750,000. If the family owns the building separately and rents it to the business for an annual rent of $200,000 when the FMV rental rate is $300,000, the resulting adjustment costs the seller another $500,000 in lost value.

Another valuation trap for a seller is that they want to hire additional sales resources to pump up their sales just prior to the sale. This is almost always a bad move. Most technology sales reps take a year or longer to ramp up to productivity. In the interim, with salary and some draw or guarantee, they actually become a drain on earnings. The buyers do not care about the explanation, they just care about the numbers and will whack you with a value downgrade.

The least understood valuation trap, however, is there seems to be no mechanism and certainly no attempt on the part of buyers to account for the selling company's growth rate. In the public market this factor is widely recognized and is accounted for with an improvement on the PE multiple, the PEG or Price Earnings Growth multiple. The rule of thumb is that if the stock is valued with a PEG of less than 1 then it is a good value and if it is over 1 it is not as good.

Because there is no exact translation between EBITDA multiple (the primary valuation metric for privately held companies) and Earnings Per Share and PE multiple (the primary valuation metric for publicly traded stocks), please allow me a measure of imprecision in my analysis. My purpose is to try to calculate an adjustment factor that can be applied against the EBITDA valuation metric in order to present a more accurate accounting for differences in growth rate for the valuation of privately held companies.

I have chosen two stocks for my analysis, Google and Facebook. The reason I choose these two is that they are widely known, very successful, in the same general market niche, and are at different stages of their growth cycle. Google sells at a PE multiple of 33.37 while Facebook sells for a PE multiple of 113.71. The PEG of Google which =

PE Multiple/5 year growth rate is 33.37/16.85 for a PEG of 1.98. I actually backed into the growth rate using the readily available PE multiple and the PEG from my Fidelity account.

Facebook sells at a PE multiple of 113.71 and has a PEG ratio of 3.62 (may be some irrational exuberance here), which translates into a 5 year growth rate of 31.41%. For our comparison we should also include the average PE multiple for the S&P 500 of about 15. Let's make the assumption that on average, this assumes that these companies will grow at the growth rate of the U.S. Economy, say 3%.

So to calculate a normalized PE ratio for these two companies, we are going to create an adjustment factor by dividing the 5 year compound growth rate of Google and Facebook versus the anticipated 5 year compound growth rate of the S&P 500. For Google the 16.85% growth rate over 5 years creates a factor or 2.178 or a total of 217.8% total growth over the next 5 years. The S&P factor is 1.16. So if you divide the Google factor by the S&P factor you get 1.878. If you multiple the market PE multiple of 15 by the Google factor, the result is a PE of 28.2. Not too far off from the current PE multiple of 33.37

Facebook is a little off using this method resulting in a normalized calculated PE of 50.65 versus their current rate of 113.71. This will appropriately seek a level over time and settle into a more rational range. My point here is that the public markets absolutely account for growth rates in the value of stocks in a very significant way.

Now let's try to apply this same logic to the EBITDA multiple for valuing a privately held technology company. If the rule-of-thumb multiple for your company's valuation is 5 X EBITDA but you are growing at 10% compounded, shouldn't you receive a premium for your company. Using the logic from above we assign a 3% compound growth rate as the norm in the 5 X EBITDA metric. So the 10% grower gets a factor of 1.61 versus the norm of 1.16. Dividing the target company factor by the normalized factor results in a multiple acceleration factor of 1.39. Multiply that by the Standard 5 X EBITDA multiple and you get a valuation metric of 6.95 X EBITDA.

A little sobering news, however, you will have a real challenge convincing a financial buyer or a Private Equity Group to veer to far away from their rule of thumb multiples. You will have a better chance of moving a strategic technology company buyer with this approach. A discounted cash flow valuation technique is superior to the rule of thumb multiple approach because it accounts for this compound growth rate in earnings. If the technique produces a higher value for the seller, the buyer will keep that valuation tool in his toolbox.

Perhaps the best way to negotiate a projected high growth rate and translate that into transaction value is with a hybrid deal structure. You might agree to a cash at close valuation of 5 X EBITDA and then create an upside kicker based on hitting your growth targets.

So for example, your EBITDA is $2 million and your standard industry metric is 5X EBITDA. You believe that your 10% growth rate (clearly above the industry average) should provide you a premium value of 6 X. So the value differential is $10 million versus $12 million. You set a target of a 10% compounded growth in Gross Profit over the next 4 years and you calculate an earn out payment methodology that would provide an additional $2 million in transaction value if you hit the targets. It is a contingent payment based on actual post closing performance, so if you fall short of targets you fall correspondingly short on your earn out. If you exceed target you could earn more.

Successful buyers do not remain as successful buyers if they over pay for an acquisition. Therefore, the lower the price they pay, the greater their odds of chalking up a win. This is a zero sum game in that each dollar that stays in their pocket is one less dollar in your pocket. They will utilize every tool at their disposal to convince the seller that "this is market" or this is "how every industry buyer values similar companies." It is to your advantage to help move them toward your value expectations. That is a very hard thing to accomplish unless you have other buyers and can walk away from a low offer. Believe me, if they are looking at you, they are doing the same dance with at least a couple of others. You must match their negotiation leverage by having your own options.

1.5 – A BUSINESS VALUATION MAY NOT ACCU-RATELY REFLECT A SOFTWARE COMPANY'S VALUE

I can't tell you the number of times I have talked with owners of software companies that are very disappointed with a valuation performed by a qualified valuation professional. The purpose of this article is not to disparage this fine profession, but to point out the limitations of a process based on quantifiable metrics. Those metrics, industry comparables or Comps, and discounted cash flow are excellent valuation approaches for most traditional businesses. In addition to these metrics, many industries have established rules of thumb for valuations like 4 X EBITDA or 70% of the trailing twelve months' revenue.

If these metrics accurately function universally over a broad range of businesses, why don't they work for software companies? The most compelling difference is the exponential nature of the leverage of technology. In its most basic form, if you are making Widgets, to make your next Widget, you need the same amount of material, labor and capital. Yes, you can achieve some economies of scale, but those improvements are linear. This limitation naturally results in a narrow range of potential business valuation multiples.

Let's compare this with the exponential scalability of software assets. Once the software is written and stress tested by a core group of users, the cost for the next unit sold is almost $0 for a digitally duplicated copy that is downloaded. To go from 100 users to 1 million users will require more staff, but it is not even close to the additional resources required for the same scaling in the manufacturing, distribution, services or retailing environment.

Software company owners that are approached by strategic buyers generally do not do a very good job of positioning their company to drive this strategic value. They will usually start with the argument that IBM or Microsoft or Google bought XYZ Competitor with $300 million in revenues for $1.2 billion. My company that is in the same space with sales of $3 million should sell for $12 million. The valuation of a large, brand name competitor is not translatable into a valuation for a small unknown company that provides a similar software. The buyers all know this and can immediately dismiss this potential seller as unrealistic.

Another limiting factor in the valuation puzzle is that finding relevant comps is very difficult with unique, small private companies. Privately held business owners do not want the public to know what they sold their company for and do not authorize the publication of that information. Unless the transaction is an acquisition by a public company and the deal value is large enough to be material and is required to be reported, no information about the transaction will be publicly available. So you can get the information on the $1.2 billion transaction but generally will not get the metrics on a $10 million deal. We are now back to the problem of the large company metrics that are not applicable to the very small company valuation.

In the discounted cash flow model, the analyst must project the cash flows out for five years and longer. To see the classic hockey stick growth actually captured in a financial model is an outlier for a typical valuation model. When a buyer analyzes this model they are generally resistant to accepting the high double digit or triple digit growth rates required to get the valuation that the owner deems appropriate.

Software company owners often put me on the spot and ask me for my opinion of value. I almost feel like the two realtors competing for a listing where the ethical guy says your house is worth $925 K and the other guy says he can get $1 million. The seller picks the $1 million realtor and then the over-priced house sits on the market for eight months before being sold for $880 K. The ethical guy could have sold it in three months for $925 K.

A software business is way more complex. Even though I am flattered that the business owner is inviting my opinion, my answer is not supportable from a classic valuation metrics standpoint. I will rely on my experience with selling similar types of companies, the level of acquisition activity happening in the space, the value of the contractually recurring revenue, the availability of similar companies that could be substituted, the uniqueness of the solution, the sales resource required to scale, the time and cost to develop the solution internally, etc. We create a teaser and a memorandum where we package and highlight the strategic value drivers to the potential buyers.

When you see these high profile technology acquisitions and see that a relative start up with no profits and limited sales was acquired for $250 million by Tech Giant A, do you think they just picked that number out and said to the seller, here you go? It looks easy and glamorous, but if the acquirer could have paid $5 million, they sure would have. What was going on behind the scenes was the equivalent of a championship boxing match of M&A. Two or more qualified firms each saw tremendous value, growth, strategic fit and potential in this prize and did whatever they could to buy it as cheaply as the market would allow.

Here are a few examples of buyer negotiation approaches to help illustrate their every attempt to make an acquisition at the lowest price possible. Well, last year your sales were unusually high. I am just going to use the average of the last three years as my number. They recognize all of their software revenue when they make the sale. I am going to adjust my bid downward by the unearned income amount. I disagree with the amount you used for the owner's replacement salary in your EBITDA analysis. I am going to put in a fair market value number to come up with this reduced EBITDA number.

If the owner is trying to sell the business himself, he can usually only process one buyer at a time and thus these buyer negotiation tactics can be very effective. Likewise, if we only have one qualified buyer, it is very difficult to negotiate off these buyer positions.

However, in a professional M&A process, we design it to process several buyer pursuits in parallel. So when a buyer tells me they are going to just normalize the last 3 years' performance to lower their bid, I do not argue with them. My response is, you are certainly entitled to whatever methodology you want to employ to come up with your offer. Unfortunately your offer is no longer competitive with the marketplace. I will present this offer to my client, but I am pretty sure he will not counter sign your Letter of Intent. So in the example above, there were several very knowledgeable and talented representatives trying to buy as cheaply as possible and the market drove the valuation to a level that no valuation model in the world could have predicted.

A competitive M&A process will provide the ultimate company valuation. The decision now becomes, is it enough for me to sell?

CHAPTER 2

Why technology business sales are unique

2.1 – An Alternative to Venture Capital for the Technology Entrepreneur

If you are an entrepreneur with a small technology based company looking to take it to the next level, this analysis should be of particular interest to you. Your natural inclination may be to seek venture capital or private equity to fund your growth. According to Jim Casparie, founder and CEO of the Venture Alliance, the odds of getting Venture funding remain below 3%. Given those odds, the six to nine month process, the heavy, often punishing valuations, the expense of the process, this might not be the best path for you to take. We have created a hybrid M&A model designed to bring the appropriate capital resources to you entrepreneurs. It allows the entrepreneur to bring in smart money and to maintain control. We have taken the experiences of several technology entrepreneurs and combined that with our traditional investment banker Merger and Acquisition approach and crafted a model that both large industry players and the high tech business owners are embracing.

Our experiences in the technology space led us to the conclusion that new product introductions were most efficiently and cost effectively the purview of the smaller, nimble, low overhead companies and not the technology giants. Most of the recent blockbuster products have been the result of an entrepreneurial effort from an early stage company bootstrapping its growth in a very cost conscious lean environment. The big companies, with all their seeming advantages experienced a high failure rate in new product introductions and the losses resulting from this art of capturing the next hot technology were substantial. Don't get us wrong.

There were hundreds of failures from the start-ups as well. However, the failure for the edgy little start-up resulted in losses in the $1 - $5 million range. The same result from an industry giant was often in the $100 million to $250 million range.

For every Google, Ebay, or Salesforce.com, there are literally hundreds of companies that either flame out or never reach a critical mass beyond a loyal early adapter market. It seems like the mentality of these smaller business owners is, using the example of the popular TV show, Deal or No Deal, to hold out for the $1 million briefcase. What about that logical contestant that objectively weighs the facts and the odds and cashes out for $280,000?

As we discussed the dynamics of this market, we were drawn to a merger and acquisition model commonly used by technology bell weather, Cisco Systems, that we felt could also be applied to a broad cross section of companies in the high tech niche. Cisco Systems is a serial acquirer of companies. They do a tremendous amount of R&D and organic product development. They recognize, however, that they cannot possibly capture all the new developments in this rapidly changing field through internal development alone.

Cisco seeks out investments in promising, small, technology companies and this approach has been a key element in their market dominance. They bring what we refer to as smart money to the high tech entrepreneur. They purchase a minority stake in the early stage company with a call option on acquiring the remainder at a later date with an agreed-upon valuation multiple. This structure is a brilliantly elegant method to dramatically enhance the risk reward profile of new product introduction. Here is why:

For the Entrepreneur: (Just substitute in your technology industry giant's name that is in your category for Cisco below)

1. The involvement of Cisco – resources, market presence, brand, distribution capability is a self fulfilling prophecy to your product's success.

2. For the same level of dilution that an entrepreneur would get from a VC, angel investor or private equity group, the entrepreneur gets the performance leverage of "smart money." See #1.

3. The entrepreneur gets to grow his business with Cisco's support at a far more rapid pace than he could alone. He is more likely to establish the critical mass needed for market leadership within his industry's brief window of opportunity.

4. He gets an exit strategy with an established valuation metric while the buyer helps him make his exit much more lucrative.

5. As an old Wharton professor used to ask, "What would you rather have, all of a grape or part of a watermelon?" That sums it up pretty well. The involvement of Cisco gives the product a much better probability of growing significantly. The entrepreneur will own a meaningful portion of a far bigger asset.

For the Large Company Investor:

1. Create access to a large funnel of developing technology and products.

2. Creates a very nimble, market sensitive, product development or R&D arm.

3. Minor resource allocation to the autonomous operator during his "skunk works" market proving development stage.

4. Diversify their product development portfolio – because this approach provides for a relatively small investment in a greater number of opportunities fueled by the entrepreneurial spirit, they greatly improve the probability of creating a winner.

5. By investing early and getting an equity position in a small company and favorable valuation metrics on the call option, they pay a fraction of the market price to what they would have to pay if they acquired the company once the product had proven successful.

Let's use two hypothetical companies to demonstrate this model, Big Green Technologies, and Mobile CRM Systems. Big Green Technologies utilized this model successfully with their investment in Mobile CRM Systems. Big Green Technologies acquired a 25% equity stake in Mobile CRM Systems in 1999 for $4 million. While allowing this entrepreneurial firm to operate autonomously, they backed them with leverage and a modest level of capital resources. Sales exploded and Big Green Technologies exercised their call option on the remaining 75% equity in Mobile CRM Systems in 2004 for $224 million. Sales for Mobile CRM Systems were projected to hit $420 million in 2005.

Given today's valuation metrics for a company with Mobile CRM Systems' growth rate and profitability, their market cap is about $1.26 Billion, or 3 times trailing 12 months revenue. Big Green Technologies invested $5 million initially, gave them access to their leverage, and exercised their call option for $224 million. Their effective acquisition price totaling $229 million represents an 82% discount to Mobile CRM Systems' 2015 market cap.

Big Green Technologies is reaping additional benefits. This acquisition was the catalyst for several additional investments in the mobile computing and content end of the tech industry. These acquisitions have transformed Big Green Technologies from a low growth legacy provider into a Wall Street standout with a growing stable of high margin, high growth brands.

Big Green Technologies' profits have tripled in four years and the stock price has doubled since 2009, far outpacing the tech industry average. This success has triggered the aggressive introduction of new products and new markets. Not bad for a $5 million bet on a new product in 2009. Wait, let's not forget about our entrepreneur. His total proceeds of $229 million are a fantastic 5- year result for a little company with 2009 sales of under $20 million.

MidMarket Capital has borrowed this model combining the Cisco hybrid acquisition experience with our investment banking experience to offer this unique Investment Banking service. MMC can either represent the small entrepreneurial firm looking for the "smart money" investment with the appropriate growth partner or the large industry player looking to enhance their new product strategy with this creative approach. This model has successfully served the technology industry through periods of outstanding growth and market value creation. Many of the same dynamics are present today in the high tech industry and these same transaction structures can be similarly employed to create value.

2.2 – Do Your Company's Sales Match the Excellence of Your Product or Service?

For many entrepreneurs, technology based companies or healthcare companies, the answer to that question is a resounding, NO! There is an exception to this with the rapid rise of the new economy, new media, highly scalable companies like Google, U-Tube, Ebay, PayPal, and Facebook. In their case, their prospective customers highly value their newness, their breaking the mold, their non-establishment approach. They are viewed as doing what they do far better than the technology establishment stalwarts. The notable exception to this is Apple who has been able to transcend old establishment and be accepted as both old and new economy.

But I digress. Back to topic. Most companies that sell to other companies, or B2B companies are evaluated by their potential customers in a traditional risk reward analysis. Or using computer terminology, their buying decisions are made using a legacy system. It was once said that no one ever got fired for making an IBM decision.

Let's look at this legacy buying model and see exactly why your company's sales do not match the elegance of your solution.

One of our healthcare clients insisted that we read CROSSING THE CHASM by Geoffrey Moore to give us greater perspective on his company's situation. By the way, if you are a smaller technology based or healthcare company selling in the B2B space, this should be required reading.

Our client was a two year old company selling a cutting edge, on-line nurse shift bidding and self scheduling system to hospitals. This is a great product. The ROI's were easily quantifiable. The handful of installed accounts loved it. Most importantly, it had a positive effect on the nursing staff's morale. This alone could justify the cost of the system.

Our client had some very encouraging early success selling his solution to some of the more progressive hospitals. They received some outstanding early PR. After that initial success, however, our little edgy technology based company hit the wall. The sales cycle went from six months to beyond twelve months. Cash flow became an issue and, to top it off, a generously funded venture backed competitor with well-known industry executives was aggressively developing this new market.

What was happening? Our clients were very smart people and figured out what was happening. They knew that they would have to make some difficult and dramatic decisions in short order. Turns out the majority of hospitals are legacy buyers and make buying decisions based on a risk avoidance paradigm. Our client's early success was realized as a result of selling to the small minority of early adapters in their industry. These are the pioneers that don't mind the arrows in their backs from heading out West with new products or new vendors.

Legacy buyers, however, do not value references that are early adapters. They are known to have a much higher risk tolerance than the traditional majority. Below are some buying criteria from these legacy buyers:

1. Big is good. Bigger is better. Buying inferior technology solutions from a blue chip publicly traded company wins most of the time.

2. Old is good. There is no replacement for experience and the grey haired company beats the gelled hair Tech Wizard company more often than not.

3. Industry Cred means everything. If you are a company that adapted your product from success in another vertical market and you are entering our space, the old familiar face carries the most weight.

4. Will the little guy be in business next year? The failure rate for the sub $ million company is a thousand times greater than for the $ billion company. This change in technology is painful enough. Do I want to risk having to do it over again in a year?

5. If I have problems, the big guy can fill the skies with blue suits until my problem is solved. The little guys cannot appropriately respond to my problem.

This is a punishing gauntlet for the small companies and it is amazing that any new companies survive in this environment. Let's look at a few of the "crossing the chasm" strategies that have been effective in swaying legacy buyers decision making in favor of the smaller provider with superior technology.

A. A well-known executive from an established healthcare company is put at the helm of the new company. The thinking from the buyer is that if he did it once, he can do it again.

B. Get an industry-recognized authority to endorse your solution or, better yet, have them join your board or advisory council.

C. Close a deal with a conservative, well respected customer and make them your marquee account with all the trimmings – i.e. a contract with a favored nations clause, the technology or computer code held in escrow with specific instructions if you go out of business, case studies and Public Relations glorifying the progressive decision maker, and providing an equity stake in your company are some examples.

D. Forging a strategic alliance, joint marketing agreement or resellers agreement with an industry giant. All of a sudden your small company risk factors have been eliminated and it has only cost you 30%-50% of revenue on each sale they make.

E. Sell your company to the best strategic buyer. Sometimes the best solution is to sell your company to the best strategic buyer for your greatest economic value. This is the most difficult decision for an entrepreneur to make. Below are some of the market dynamics that would point to that decision. Note: several of these factors influenced our entrepreneurial clients to ultimately sell their business to an industry giant.

You see your window of opportunity closing rapidly. You may have great technology and the market is starting to recognize the value of the solution. However, you have a small competitor that was just acquired by a big industry player. The bad news is you probably have to sell to remain competitive. The good news is that the market will likely bid up the value of your company to offset the competitive move of the big buyer.

The strategic alliance is with the right company, but the sales force has no sense of urgency or no focus on selling your product. The large company lacks the commitment to drive your sales. An amazing thing happens with an acquisition. The CEO is out to prove that his decision was the right one. He will make his decision right. All of a sudden there is laser focus on integrating this new product and driving sales.

You have created a strategic alliance and poured your company's resources into educating, supporting, and evangelizing your product. Whoops, you have counted on this golden goose and it has not met your expectations. Also you have neglected your other business development and sales efforts while focusing on this partner.

Many large healthcare companies now employ a try it before you buy it approach to M&A. They find a good technology, formalize a strategic alliance, dangle the carrot of massive distribution and expect the small company to educate and integrate with his sales force. Often this relationship drains the financial performance of the smaller company. If you decide to sell at this point your value to another potential buyer has been diminished.

Do not despair. If you have demonstrated a cultural fit and have helped your products work in conjunction with the big company's product suite, you have largely eliminated post acquisition integration risk. This can often more than offset any short-term profit erosion you may have suffered.

It is not easy for the smaller healthcare company to reach critical mass in this very competitive and conservative environment. Working harder will not necessarily get you where you need to be. Step back and look at your environment through the eyes of your buyers. Implement some of these strategies to remove the risk barriers to doing business with your company. Now you have created an opportunity for your sales to match the elegance of your technology solution.

2.3 – Grow or Sell Your Information Technology Company: A Crossroads Decision

Thinking of taking your information technology company to the next level with a major marketing campaign or by hiring additional sales resources? These are decisions that can impact your company's future. It might be time to consider the alternative of selling your business.

We are often approached by software company or information technology business owners at a crossroads of taking the company to the next level. The decision in most cases is whether they should bring on the one or two hot shot sales people or channel development people necessary to bring the company sales to a level that will allow the company to reach critical mass. For a smaller company with sales below $5 million this can be a critical decision.

For frame of reference, prior to embarking on my merger and acquisition advisor career, I spent my prior 20 years in various sales capacities in primarily information technology and computer industry related companies from bag carrying salesman to district, regional, to national sales manager and finally Chief Marketing Officer. So when I look at a company, it is from the sales and marketing perspective first and foremost. I am sure that if I had a public accounting background, I would look at my clients through those lenses.

So with that backdrop, let's look at what might be a typical situation. The software company is doing $7.5 million in sales, has a good group of loyal customers, produces a nice income for its owner or owners, and has a lot more potential for sales growth in the opinion of the owner. Some light bulb has been lit that suggests that they need to step this up to the next level after relying on word of mouth and the passion and energy of the owner to get to this stage.

I have spoken with more than 50, primarily technology based companies over the years that have faced this exact situation and can count on one hand the ones that had a successful outcome. The natural inclination is to bite the bullet and bring on that expensive resource and hope your staff can keep up with the big influx of orders. The reality is that in most cases the execution was a very expensive failure. Below are several factors that you should consider when you are at this crossroads:

1. The 80 20 rule of salesmen. You know this one. 80% of sales are produced by 20% of the salespeople. If you are only hiring one or two, the likelihood is that you will not get a top performer.

2. The president of the company and deci-

sion maker has no sales background so the odds of him making the right hiring decision are greatly diminished. He will not understand how to properly set milestones, judge progress, evaluate performance objectively, or coach the new hire.

3. To hire a good salesman that can handle a complex sale requires a base salary and a draw for at least 6 months that puts him in a better economic condition than he was in on his last job. So you are probably looking at $150,000 annual run rate for a decent candidate.

4. If you have not had a formalized sales effort before, you are probably lacking the sales infrastructure that your new hire is used to. Proper contact management systems, customer and prospect databases, developed collateral materials and sales presentations, sales cycle timeframes and critical milestones and developed competition feature benefit matrixes will need to be developed.

5. Current customers are most likely the early adapters, risk takers, pioneers, etc. and are not afraid of making the buying decision with a small more risky company. These early adaptors, however, are not viewed as good references for the more conservative majority that needs the security of a big company backing their product selection decision.

6. Your new hire is most likely someone that came from a bigger information technology company and may be comfortable performing in an established sales department. It is the rare salesman that can transform from that environment to developing the environment while trying to meet a sales quota. Throw on top of that the objection that he has never had to deal with before, the small company risk factor, and the odds of success diminish. Finally, this transformation from a core group of early adapters to now selling to the conservative majority elongates the sales cycle by 25% to as much as double his prior experience. If you don't fire him first, he will probably quit when his draw runs out.

With all this going against the business owner, most of them go ahead and make the hire and then I hear something like this, "Yes, we brought on a sales guy two years ago who said he had all the industry contacts and in nine months after he hadn't sold a thing and cost us a lot of money, we fired him. That really hurt the company and we have just now recovered. We won't do that again."

What are the alternatives? Certainly strategic alliances, channel partnerships, value added resellers are options, but again the success rate for these arrangements are suspect without the sales background in the executive suite. A lower risk approach is to outsource your VP of Sales or Chief Marketing Officer function. There are a number of highly experienced and talented free lancers that you can hire on a consulting basis that can help you establish a sales and marketing infrastructure and guide you through the staffing process. That may be the best way to go.

An option that one of our clients chose when faced with the six points to consider from above was to sell his company. This is a very difficult decision for an entrepreneur who by nature is very optimistic about the future and feels like he can clear any hurdle. This client had no sales background but was a very smart subject matter expert with an outstanding background as a former consultant with a Big 5 accounting firm. He did not make the hiring mistake, but instead went the outsourcing of VP of Sales function as step 1. When their firm wanted to make the transition from the early adapters to the conservative majority, the sales cycle slowed to a crawl. Meanwhile their technology advantage was being eroded by a well funded venture backed competitor that had struck an alliance with a big vendor.

They engaged our firm to find them a buyer, but then we encountered the valuation gap. Our business seller thought his company was worth a great deal and that he should be paid with cash at close for all the future potential his product could deliver. The buyer, on the other hand, wanted to pay based on a trailing twelve months historical perspective and if anything was paid for potential, that would be in the form of an earn out based on post acquisition sales performance.

With a well structured earn out agreement and the right buyer, our client will reach his transaction value goals. His earn out is based on future sales, but his effective sales force has been increased from one (himself) to 27 reps. His install base has been increased from 14 to

800. Every one of the buyer's current customers is a candidate for this product. The small company risk has been removed going from a little known start-up with $3.5 million in revenues to a well known industry player, publicly traded stock with a market cap of $2.5 billion.

He avoided the big cash drain that a bad sales person hiring decision would have created and he sold his company before a competitor dominated the market and made his technology irrelevant and of minimal value.

My professional contacts sometimes tease me and suggest that I think every company should be sold. That may be a slight exaggeration, but in many instances, a company sale is the best route. When a information technology business owner is faced with that crossroads decision of bringing on a significant sales resource that will be faced with a complex sale and the executive suite does not have the sales background, a company sale may be the best outcome.

2.4 – Capturing That Elusive Strategic Value in a Business Sale

Wow did I get a real world demonstration of the saying, "Beauty is in the eyes of the beholder." If I could rephrase that to the business sale situation it could be, Strategic Value is in the eyes of the particular buyer." We are representing a small company that has a patented and somewhat unique product. They have gotten distribution in several hardware store chains, Lowes, and are going into Wal*Mart next spring.

The owners are at a cross-roads. To keep up with their growth in volume they recognize that they require a substantial capital investment. They understand that they have a window of opportunity to achieve a meaningful footprint before a much better capitalized competitor produces a similar product and undercuts their price. Finally they realize that a one product company at a big box retailer is quite vulnerable to the inevitable rotation of buyers or a change in policy that bumps them out of 25% of their sales volume.

The good news is that their product is unique and is protected for 15 more years with utility patents. It is not a commodity so it achieves healthy margins. The product is an eco friendly product so the retailers value that. Finally, the product can be used in retailer programs where it is combined with other same category products for the spring tune up and the fall tune up. It helps drive the sales of other products.

The ideal company buyer is a larger company that provides products in the same category and sells to the same retailers. They could plug this product into their existing distribution channel and immediately drive additional sales. They would strengthen their position within their accounts by offering an additional product, a unique product, an eco friendly product, and a product that would promote companion product sales. It would also provide a unique door opener to other major accounts that would want this unique product.

With the input from our clients we located a handful of companies that fit this profile. We were pretty excited at the prospects of our potential buyers recognizing all of these value drivers and making purchase offers that were not based on historical financial performance. The book, memorandum, confidential business review, executive summary, or whatever your business broker or merger and acquisition advisor calls it, will certainly point out all of the strategic value that this company can provide the company that is lucky enough to buy it.

As part of the buying process we usually distribute the book and then get a round of additional questions from the buyer. We submit those to our client and then provide the answers to the buyer with a request for a conference call. We had moved the process to this point with two buyers that we thought were similar companies. The two conference calls were totally different.

The first one included the Merger and Acquisition guy and the three top people responsible for the product category. Their questions really indicated that they were used to being leveraged as a commodity provider by the big box retailers. Why were co-op advertising costs so high? Were they required to do that again in order to stay on the shelves? Were they on the plan-o-gram? Was Wal*Mart demanding that they be at a lower price than Lowes? What about shipping expenses? Why were profits so low? We had a very bad vibe from these guys. They were refusing to recognize that this was a high gross margin product growing in sales by over 200% year over year and had a higher level of promotional expense than a mature commodity product line. We couldn't determine if they just didn't get it or were they being dumb like a fox to dampen our value expectations.

The second call from the other company included the Merger and Acquisition guy and the EVP.

The whole tone of the questioning was different. The questions focused on growth in sales, pricing power, new client potential, growth strategy, their status at the major accounts, remaining life on the patent and what their strategy was for new categories and markets.

Well we got the initial offers and they could not have been more different. The first company could not get beyond evaluating the acquisition as if it were a mature, commodity type product with paper thin margins. Their offer was an EBITDA multiple bid without taking into consideration that the product sales had grown at over 200% year over year and the marketing and promotional expenses were heavily front end loaded.

The second company understood the strategic value and they reflected it in the offer. It was not an apples to apples comparison, because the second offer was cash at close plus a significant earn out component while the first offer was all cash at close. However, the conservative mid-point of the combined cash and earn out offer was 300% higher than the offer from the first buyer. This was the biggest disparity between offers I have ever experienced, but it was quite instructive of the necessity to get multiple opinions by the market of potential buyers.

There are some companies that no matter how hard we try will not be perceived as a strategic acquisition by any buyer and they are going to sell at a financial multiple. Those companies are often main street type companies like gas stations, convenience stores and dry cleaners that are acquired by individual buyers. If you are a B2B company, have a competitive niche, and are not selling into a commodity type pricing structure, it is important to get multiple buyers involved and to get at least one of those buyers to acknowledge the strategic value.

2.5 – Gentlemen, So How Much Do You Want for Your Software Company

I will never forget this scene. We were in the board room of a one billion market cap NYSE traded company representing our client, a small software company. We thought we were going to meet with the general manager and his team from the $100 million division that was going to utilize our client's product. In walks the Executive Vice President and after some brief introductions he says, "Gentlemen, so how much do you want for your company?'

I looked over at our clients and watched as the color drained from their faces. They looked back at me as if to say, O.K., Dave, this would be where you step in. Taking the hint, I started down the path of suggesting that we wanted to understand the synergies between the two companies. I was quickly taken off my course with the EVP saying, "I appreciate what you are trying to do, but how much do you want for your business?"

It was almost lunchtime and I knew that they had ordered sandwiches for a working lunch. I requested that we huddle separately and that we could reconvene after lunch. After they left us, I said to our clients, I know exactly what is going on here. This guy is trying to quickly determine whether these entrepreneurs are realistic in their expectations and will be worth continuing discussions or whether they should catch the next plane back to Chicago.

This situation was complicated by the fact that we had other interested buyers, but were early in the process and had no other offers thus far. This buyer was the number one strategic buyer. In other words, they are the company that can create the most economic value in the three years following the acquisition. That is impacted by such factors as how close the new product meshes with their existing product suite, how many installed accounts they have, the number of salesmen, etc. Finally, we were going to be seeking a transaction value that would not be supported by any traditional valuation models. We were seeking an aggressive strategic value.

We generally like the buyer to offer first, but the EVP was making that very difficult. The worst thing that could happen to us is that we say we want $5 million and he immediately responds, we'll take it! It is almost impossible to negotiate up from there. So our challenge was to come up with a number and deal structure that did not short change our owners while not scaring off the buyers.

We had done our research and found that our client's product was a logical add-on to their existing product that was installed in approximately 1100 accounts. They were getting pressure from a well funded venture backed company that had a similar product and also had designs of displacing the buyer's core offering. This new product category was getting a lot of attention from other major competitors as well.

Emboldened by this information and bolstered

with our analysis of factors such as:

Time to Market

Window of Opportunity

Development Cost

Brand Name Pricing Leverage (a big company can charge 25%-50% more for the
identical product)

Potential Customer Base Defection

We made our pitch, discussed these points, and
presented our value and deal structure request. Then
we held our breath. The EVP, a tough but charis-
matic New Zealander looked at us and said, "That's
outrageous, but not bloody outrageous. Let's talk."
Well we caught the late flight back to Chicago that
night with a commitment for a qualified letter of
intent within the next three business days.

We still had a lot of work left, but the ground-
work was set for productive negotiations, due diligence and a completed sale.

CHAPTER 3

Driving strategic Value in Your Company Sale

3.1 – Ten Steps To Maximize Your Selling Price

You started your company 20 years ago "in your garage", worked many 80 hour weeks, bootstrapped your growth, view your company with the pride of an entrepreneur, and are now considering your exit. Our purpose is to help you evaluate your company as a strategic acquirer might. From that perspective we will ask you to focus on ten critical areas of value creation. The benefit to you is that the better your performance in these areas, the greater the selling price of your business. The most likely result is that you will sell at the high range of the multiples normally associated with your industry. For example, during the last 18 months similar companies have sold at an EBITDA multiple of between 4.8 and 5.7 times. Moving your company from the low end to the high end of that range can result in a significant swing in transaction value. If your EBITDA were $2 million, the low price is $9.6 million and the high price is $11.4 million. The Holy Grail in selling your company is when an acquirer throws out the traditional multiples and acquires your company based on strategic post acquisition performance. Below is our list of STRATEGIC VALUE DRIVERS:

1. CUSTOMER DIVERSITY – If too much of your current business is concentrated in too few customers that is perceived as a negative in the acquisition market. The concern is that if the owner exits and the major customers leave, the business could be negatively impacted. On the plus side, if none of your customers accounts for more than 5% of total sales, that is viewed as a real plus. If you find yourself with a customer concentration issue and are planning an exit, start focusing on a program to diversify. A quick fix would be to make an acquisition of a competitor with customer diversity, integrate them and then take your company to market.

2. MANAGEMENT DEPTH – A common thread in privately held businesses is a concentration of responsibility with the owner operator. The buck stops here may be a good slogan for a presidential candidate, but it will not help create value for a business owner. An acquirer will look at the quality of the management staff and employees as a major determinant in acquisition price. A key in preparing for exit is to develop your people so they could run the business after you are gone. You should make the move of assigning your successor a year in advance of your scheduled departure date. If you have no one that you feel has the ability then go hire someone that can do the job. If you have a strong management team in place and you are anticipating an exit, you should try to implement employment contracts, non-competes, and some form of phantom stock or equity participation plan to keep these stars involved through the transition. A strong management team is a valuable asset in the middle market. If you have one, take steps to keep it in place and the market will reward you. If you are weak in that area, the acquisition market will punish you if fail to take the corrective action.

3. CONTRACTUALLY RECURRING REVENUE – All revenue dollars are not created equal. Revenue dollars that are the result of a contract for annual maintenance, annual licensing fees, a recurring retainer fee, technology license, etc. are much more powerful value drivers than new sales revenue, time and materials revenue, or other non-recurring revenue streams. It's all about risk. The higher the risk (future sales) the lower the return. The lower the risk (contracted revenue stream) the higher the return. The most extreme case of this occurs in the software industry where companies are typically sold at a multiple of recurring maintenance revenue. New license sales, historical levels of project work and projected install revenue are virtually eliminated from the valuation formula. The lesson here is that if you can turn a T&M situation into an annual contract, you will be greatly rewarded when it comes time to sell your business.

4. PROPRIETARY PRODUCTS/TECHNOLOGY – This is the area where the valuation rules do not necessarily apply. Strategic acquirers buy other companies to grow. If they believe that a new technology can be acquired and integrated with their superior distribution channel, they may value your company on a post acquisition performance basis. The marketplace rewards effective innovation. On the flip side, however, the market yawns at "me too" commodity type products or services. That business is vulnerable to competition, especially after the owner leaves. Continue to look for ways to innovate in what ever industry you are in. Your innovation should not be limited to product improvements. The marketplace values innovations in distribution systems, collaborative product design process, customer service and other functional areas that can provide a competitive advantage. If you create a technology advantage in your company, think what that could mean to a much larger company.

5. PENETRATION OF BARRIERS TO ENTRY – A wise buyer told me once, "I want to own companies where I have an edge." He happened to be a buyer of Waste Facilities. All the regulations and approvals required tend to limit competition. In its simplest form, a large restaurant chain buys a small family owned restaurant to acquire a grand fathered liquor license. Owning hard to get permits, zoning, licenses, or regulatory approvals can be worth a great deal to the right buyer. Your company may be able to secure approvals on the local level that a national player may have difficulty obtaining. Selling your product or service to the government can be quite lucrative, but the government market is extremely difficult to penetrate. If your product or service applies and you can break through the barriers, you become a more attractive acquisition candidate. The same holds true of a local marquee account that would be desirable for a larger supplier to crack. One strategy for penetrating these accounts is to ask the buyer to identify the best salesman that calls on him. Go hire that salesman to sell your product to that account.

6. EFFECTIVE USE OF PROFESSIONALS – Reviewed or audited financials by a reputable CPA firm are quite valuable in the eyes of a buyer. Professional financials cast a positive halo on your approach to controlling your business while at the same time reduce the buyer's perception of risk. Bring a good outside attorney into the mix, and the risk drops even more. The thought process is that this attorney has been giving his client good advice for years on protecting the company from litigation. A strong professional team is a great asset in growing your business and in helping you obtain maximum value when you exit.

7. PRODUCT/SALES PIPELINE – Large pharmaceutical companies are well known for buying smaller pharmaceutical companies that have a robust product pipeline for very generous prices. Smaller companies often are more agile and have better R&D efficiency than their high overhead big brothers. In technology, time to market is critical and big companies are constantly evaluating the build versus buy question. Small companies that develop a hot new technology are faced with the decision of developing distribution internally or selling to a larger company with developed channels. A win/win scenario is to sell out at a price, in cash and stock at closing, that rewards the smaller company for what they have today, plus an earn out component tied to product revenues with the new company. The same earn out philosophy can be employed for a selling company that has a large sales pipeline. The acquirer is not anxious to pay for that pipeline at closing and the seller wants to delay his company's sale until the next big deal. An intelligently structured sales contract with a contingent payment based on closing accounts in the pipeline is a great solution.

8. PRODUCT DIVERSITY – A smaller company that has a quality portfolio of products but may lack distribution can become a valuable asset in the hands of the strategic buyer. A narrow product set, however, increases risk and drives down value. If you are planning to exit, review your product portfolio. Are there obvious gaps that could be filled quickly? How about buying a small company with a few complementary products? What about buying a product line from a company? Can you lock up distribution rights for North America for the best product from a Finnish manufacturer? Have your customers been asking you to develop a new product? Spread out your product risk as a value enhancing strategy.

9. INDUSTRY EXPERTISE AND EXPOSURE – This activity is often overlooked because it is difficult to measure its direct returns. We find that it is a value driver when it is time to sell the business. To the extent possible, encourage your staff to publish articles in industry magazines and newsletters. Get exposure as a presenter at industry events. Encourage local and industry reporters to use you as the voice of authority with industry issues. Your company is viewed in a more positive light, you may get more business referrals, and a buyer from your industry will remember you favorably and is more likely to consider you as an acquisition candidate.

10. WRITTEN GROWTH PLAN – If I could get you to do one thing that will cost you nothing but brain power and your time it would be to capture the opportunities available to your company in a two to five page written growth plan. Even if you are putting your company on the market tomorrow, it is not too late to identify all the opportunities your company has created. For any company, in any stage, this is a valuable living document to guide you strategically. Small companies with limited staff are forced to put out fires and live tactically. A growth plan helps create a process that will allow you to break big strategic plans into executable tactical activities. What additional markets could we pursue? What additional products could we deliver to our same customers? What segments of my current market offer the most growth potential? Where are the best margins in our customer set and product set? Can we expand in those areas? Can we repurpose our products for different markets? Are we getting the best return on our intellectual property? Can we license our technology? Do strategic alliances or cross marketing agreements make sense? Capturing this on paper as part of your exit plan will increase the likelihood that an acquiring company will view you more as a strategic acquisition. It demonstrates that you have identified a path for growth and it may identify opportunities that the buyer had not considered. Those opportunities can add to the purchase price.

The bottom line when it comes to unlocking the market value of your privately held company is not limited to the bottom line. Profitability is hugely important, but the factors above can result in significant premiums over traditional valuation approaches. When one buys or sells Microsoft stock, there is no room for interpretation about the market price. The market for privately held businesses is imprecise and illiquid. There is plenty of room for interpretation and the result for the best interpretation by the marketplace is a big pay off when you decide to sell.

3.2 – How You Sell Your Business Determines its Selling Price

How much is my business worth? That depends. Of course it depends on profits, sales, EBITDA, and other traditional valuation metrics. A surprisingly important factor, however, is how you choose to sell it. If your business is larger, complex, unusual, strategic, with a high component of intellectual property or technology and subject to a broad interpretation of value in the marketplace then how you choose to sell it can result in swings of literally millions of dollars in transaction value. The Graph below attempts to illustrate this concept:

The way to achieve the most value from the sale of your company is to get several strategic buyers all competing in a soft auction process. That is the holy grail of company valuation. There are several exit or value options. Let's examine each one starting with the lowest which is liquidation value.

Liquidation Value – This is basically the sale of the hard assets of the business as it ceases to be a going concern. No value is given for good will, brand name, customer lists, or company earnings capability. This is a sad way to exit a business that you spent twenty years building. This method of selling often occurs when the owner has a debilitating health issue or dies and his estate is forced to sell.

Book Value - is simply an accounting treatment of the physical assets. Book value is generally not even close to the true value of a business. It only accounts for the depreciated value of physical assets and does not take into account such things as earnings power, proprietary technology, competitive advantage, growth rate, and many other important factors. In case you are working on a shareholder agreement and looking for a methodology for calculating a buy-out, Book value is a terrible metric to use. A better approach would be a multiple of sales or EBITDA. Minority shareholders often unknowingly sign shareholder agreements that provide a book value buyout if the minority shareholder decides to cash out.

<u>Unsolicited Offer to Buy from a Competitor</u> – This is the next step up in value. The best way I can describe the buyer mindset is that they are hoping to get lucky and buy your company for a bargain price. If the unsuspecting seller bites or makes a weak counter offer, the competitor gets a great deal.

How should you handle this situation so you do not have this outcome? We suggest that you do not let an outside force determine your selling timeframe. However, we recognize that everything is for sale at the right price. That is the right starting point. Get the buyer to sign a confidentiality agreement. Provide income statement, balance sheet and your yearly budget and forecast.

Determine the number that you would accept as your purchase price and present that to the buyer. You may put it like this, " We really were not considering selling our company, but if you want us to consider going through the due diligence process, we will need an offer of $6.5 million. If you are not prepared to give us a LOI at that level, we are not going to entertain further discussions."

A second approach would be to ask for your

number and if they were willing to agree, then you would agree to begin the due diligence process. If they were not, then you were going to engage your merger and acquisition advisor and they would be welcome to participate in the process with the other buyers that were brought into the competitive selling process.

Another tactic from this bargain seeker it to propose a reasonable offer in a qualified letter of intent and then embark on an exhaustive due diligence process. He uncovers every little flaw in the target company and begins the process of chipping away at value and lowering his original purchase offer. He is counting on the seller simply wearing down since the seller has invested so much in the process and accepting the significantly lower offer.

Buyer Introduced by Seller's Professional Advisors – Unfortunately this is a commonly executed yet flawed approach to maximizing the seller's transaction value. The seller confides in his banker, financial advisor, accountant, or attorney that he is considering selling. The well-meaning advisor will often "know a client in the same business" and will provide an introduction. This introduction often results in a bidding process of only one buyer. That buyer has no motivation to offer anything but a discounted price.

<u>Valuation From a Professional Valuation Firm</u> – At about the midpoint in the value chain is this view of business value. These valuations are often in response to a need such as gift or estate taxes, setting up an ESOP, a divorce, insurance, or estate planning. These valuations are conservative and are generally done strictly by the numbers. These firms use several techniques, including comps, rules of thumb, and discounted cash flow. These methods are not great in accounting for strategic value factors such as key customers, intellectual capital, or a competitive bidding process from several buyers.

<u>Private Equity or Financial Buyer</u> – In this environment of tight credit, the Private Equity Groups still have a good amount of capital and need to invest in deals. The very large deals are not currently getting done, but the lower middle market transactions are still viable. The PEG's still have their roots as financial buyers and go strictly by the numbers, and they have tightened the multiples they are willing to pay. Where two years ago they would buy a bricks and mortar company for 6 ½ X EBITDA, they are now paying 5 X EBITDA.

Strategic Buyers in a Bidding Process – The Holy Grail of transaction value for business sellers is to have several buyers that are actively seeking to acquire the target company. One of the luckiest things that has happened in our client's favor as they were engaged in selling their company was an announcement that a big company just acquired one of the seller's competitors. All of a sudden our client became a strategic prized target for the competitors of the buying company. If for no other reason than to protect market share, these buyers come out of the woodwork with some very aggressive offers.

This principal holds as an M&A firm attempts to stimulate the same kind of market dynamic. By positioning the seller as a potential strategic target of a competitor, the other industry players often step up with attractive valuations in a defensive posture.

Another value driver that a good investment banker will employ is to establish a strategic fit between seller and buyer. The advisor will attempt to paint a picture of 1 + 1 = 3 ½. Factors such as eliminating duplication of function, cross selling each other's products into the other's install base, using the seller's product to enhance the competitive position of the buying company's key products, and extending the life of the buyer's technology are examples of this artful positioning.

Of course, the merger and acquisition teams of the buyers are conditioned to deflect these approaches. However, they realize that their competitors are getting the same presentation. They have to ask themselves, "Which of these strategic platforms will resonate with their competitors' decision makers?"

As you can see, the value of your business can be subjectively interpreted depending on the lenses through which it is viewed. The decision you make on how your business is sold will determine how value is interpreted and can result in 20%, 30%, 40%, or even 100% differences in your sale proceeds.

3.3 – The Number One Driver of Business Valuation in a Software Company Sale

We get to witness buyer behavior first hand in our software investment banking practice. The most important behavior is their economic vote – how much they are willing to pay for an information technology business. Many factors go into their assessment of value, but a contractually recurring revenue stream is consistently the number one value driver.

Why is this so important? The first answer is risk. Buying a business is risky. Any factor that reduces this risk is rewarded with transaction value. Forecasted sales, for example, are at the high end of the risk scale and are heavily discounted in value. Historical time and materials revenues that are "most likely to be at about the same level" next year are somewhere in the middle of the risk scale and are valued accordingly.

The owner and key employees may leave after the acquisition and may take their customer relationships and accounts with them. Those customers locked into contracts are less likely to leave. The acquisition can temporarily inject uncertainty into the marketplace and cause disruption or delays in pending sales situations. The integration efforts will introduce execution risk into previously routine revenue generating activities.

The acquiring company wants the existing customers to stay put long enough to get comfortable with the new company. Contracts with plenty of time remaining are their security.

How can you use this knowledge to your advantage? Here are some actions the owners should take in anticipation of selling their software or information technology business. Many of these actions would be implemented by the acquirer post acquisition. If, you implement them prior to the sale, the buyers will reflect that in an enhanced purchase price. If the buyer implements them post acquisition, they certainly will not pay you for the improvements.

Go on a mission to convert every time and materials revenue source you can to an annual contract. If you are a software company, for example, and you have customers that are not on an 18% - 20% annual maintenance contract, get those customers converted. A strategy might be a one time "get current sale" in return for signing an annual maintenance contract. Services companies should review their T & M records with their regular customers and devise programs that convert those to annual fixed price programs. Software companies that also provide services, devise a concept where you provide departmental or functional outsourcing for your clients.

Review all long-term maintenance contracts and implement price increases that are covered by your annual increase limits. Send your sales team out to all accounts that are not on your latest version. Bring those accounts current with the appropriate license and maintenance level increase.

Do you have any Add-on modules that your customer base has been slow to adopt? Offer a 2-year price freeze on their currently installed software if they buy the add-on module and sign a maintenance agreement. The principal theme of these actions is to increase your company's level of contractually recurring revenue. That is your most important financial driver of the value of your company.

Tie these actions directly to your sales team's commission plan. The commission plan should tell your sales reps exactly what you value. A higher commission rate should be applied to recurring revenue contracts. If you have poor performers, immediately put them on notice. You may tie their future employment to meeting some short-term goals in these strategic areas. If they continue to under perform, let them go. A buyer that is looking at your business will rightfully question your management capability when the find in due diligence that you have allowed a poor performer to drain profits from your company.

If you are concerned that firing the sales rep would be disruptive to your customer base, offer to allow him to stay on a commission only plan. Remove his fixed salary portion and replace that with a higher commission rate that would equal his previous expected compensation level at 100% of quota. Let's think of it this way. If a salesman's lack of performance is costing you $50,000 in EBITDA and your company will sell at a 7 X multiple, this laggard will cost you $350,000 in transaction value.

Your key short-term strategy in maximizing your company's value in the marketplace is to increase the level of contractually recurring revenue. As an acquiring company looks at you as a potential acquisition target they place a value of, for example, 1 X on projected new sales supported by historical performance. They will place a value of 2 X on the revenue that is covered by contracts they acquire with the purchase of your information technology company.

On a value scale, contractually recurring revenue is a 10, expected historical revenue is a 6 and a sales pipeline is a 3. Move your 3's and 6's to 10's and recognize a big boost in your business selling price.

Go on a Contractually Recurring Revenue Hunt Before you Sell your Information Technology Company.

3.4 – CREATING COMPANY VALUE THROUGH STRATEGIC ACQUISITIONS

Successful growing companies usually grow through a combination of organic growth and strategic acquisitions. For purposes of this analysis, a strategic acquisition is defined as an acquisition where the result of the combination is far greater than the sum of the parts. For example, if Company A with revenues of $50 million Acquires Company SA with revenues of $10 million, the Newco mathematically would have revenues of $60 million. The anticipated performance of a well thought out strategic purchase might result in a combined revenue for Newco of $100 million within a 1 to 2 year period. A second category of strategic acquisition would focus on an improvement of the profit margins of Newco.

Let's use two companies that are recognized as among the best at making successful acquisitions, General Electric and Cisco Systems. As their stockholders will happily tell you, these companies have been star performers in growing shareholder value. General Electric is a giant conglomerate with business lines such as GE Capital, GE Plastics, GE Power Systems,

GE Medical, and several others. Cisco Systems could be categorized as a high tech growth company primarily focusing on voice and data communications hardware, software, and services.

The first rule of strategic acquisition we learn from these two prolific and successful companies is that they do it on purpose. They have a well thought out defined approach. To quote GE, "We are allocating capital to businesses that can increase growth with higher returns, businesses requiring human capital as opposed to physical capital. We are disciplined and integrators and we grow the businesses we acquire. Over the past 10 years Cisco Systems has acquired 81 companies. If you track their stock price over the same period, it is up a remarkable 1300% over that same period. GE, starting with a much larger base, still outperformed the S&P 500 index over the same period 3 to 1.

If you study the acquisitions of these two companies as well as good middle market growth through acquisition companies, you find some common strategic themes. The core principal that runs through almost every example is INTEGRATION. With the exception of establishing the original platform, GE expanding from their original roots and establishing a presence in plastics, for example, all of these acquisitions focus on integration.

An example that I use to summarize strategic acquisitions for Cisco Systems is not a real acquisition, but a hypothetical company that should demonstrate a point. I have been a very happy stockholder for over a decade. It seems like every year they would announce an acquisition that looked like this – Today Cisco announced the acquisition of Optical Solutions Company for $30 million in stock. Optical Solutions Company manufactures the OptiFast Switch, the fastest optical networking switch on the market today. The Company was started two years ago by two Stanford Electrical Engineering Professors. Current sales are $1.5 million and last year they lost $700,000. My initial reaction was, "What the heck are they doing?" What they were really looking at was what this technology could become as it was integrated into the Cisco family. First, Cisco has 5,000 sales reps, 12,000 value added resellers and systems integrators that sell their solutions, and 600,000 customers that think Cisco walks on water. Cisco knows their market, their customers, and the first mover advantage in their market.

With this backdrop, the OptiFast Switch achieves sales of $130 million in its second year of Cisco sales. That's what the heck they were doing – a classic strategic acquisition.

There are several categories of strategic acquisition that can produce some outstanding results with effective integration. Many acquisitions actually have elements from several categories.

1. Acquire Customers – this is almost always a factor in strategic acquisitions. Some companies buy another that is in the same business in a different geography. They get to integrate market presence, brand awareness, and market momentum. Another approach is to acquire a company that can establish a presence for you in a different market segment. For example, let's say that that Company A made fasteners for the automotive industry and felt that their expertise could be applied to the aerospace industry. A company that produced fasteners for the target industry could help jump-start this strategic initiative.

2. Operating Leverage – the major focus in this type of acquisition is to improve profit margins through higher utilization rates for plant and equipment. A manufacturer of cardboard containers that is operating at 65% of capacity buys a smaller similar manufacturer. The acquired company's plant is sold, all but two machines are sold, the G&A staff are let go and the new customers are served more cost effectively. Adding new customers without increasing fixed expenses results in higher profit margins.

3. Valuation Multiple Expansion – this is a subtle mathematical approach that the private equity groups understand very well and regularly capitalize upon. They establish a platform company, usually in the $30 million to $250 million in revenue range and then they go on a mission to acquire several "tuck in acquisitions". They buy several other companies that can add to the value of the platform company based on expanding the customer base, improving on their technology, broadening their product line, or other strategic point covered in this article. They also recognize that a small company will sell at a smaller valuation multiple than their larger platform company.

Below is an example of how that might work for a company looking to grow through acquisitions. Let's say that the acquiring company is $30 million in revenue and is looking to acquire a $10 million in revenue target. The $30 million company with $7.5 million in EBITDA has a valuation multiple of 6.5 X EBITDA while the $10 million company with $2.5 million in EBITDA has a multiple of 5.25 X EBITDA. Pre acquisition that would mean that the value of the acquirer was $48.75 million and the target was $13.125 million. Theoretically, if you combined the two companies, the new value should be $48.75 plus $13.125 or $61.875 million. However, post acquisition, the combined company takes on the EBITDA multiple of the acquiring company resulting in a valuation of ($2.5 + $7.5 million in EBITDA) or $10 million X 6.5 or $65 million. Wall Street refers to this phenomenon as an accretive acquisition

4. Capitalize on a company strength – this is why Cisco and GE have been so successful with their acquisitions. They are so strong in so many areas, that the acquired company gets the benefit of some, if not all of those strengths. A very powerful business accelerator is to acquire a company that has a complementary product that is used by your installed customer base. It is ten times easier to sell an add-on product to an installed account than to sell a product to a new account. Management depth and skill, production efficiency/capacity, large base of installed accounts, developed sales and distribution channels, and brand recognition are examples of strengths that can power post acquisition performance.

5. Cover a Weakness – This requires a good deal of objectivity from the acquiring company in recognizing and chinks in the corporate armor. Let me help you with some suggestions – 1. Customer concentration: too much of your business is concentrated on a small group of customers 2. Product concentration: too much of your business is the result of one or two products 3. Weak product pipeline – in a business environment that is becoming more innovation focused, having a thin product pipeline could be fatal. Many of the acquisitions in the pharmaceutical industry are aimed at covering this weakness. 4. Management depth or technical expertise and 5. Great technology and products – poor sales and marketing.

6. Buy a Low Cost Supplier – this integration strategy is typically aimed at improving profit margins rather than growing revenues. If your product is comprised of several manufactured components, one way to improve corporate profitability is to acquire one of those suppliers. You achieve greater control of overall costs, availability of supply, and greater value-add to your end product. Another variation of this theme some refer to as horizontal integration is to acquire a company supplying you distribution.

7. Improving or Completing a Product

Line – this approach has several elements from other acquisition strategies. Successfully adding new products to a line improves profitability and revenue growth. Giving a sales force more "arrows in their quiver" is a powerful growth strategy. You take advantage of your existing sales and distribution channel (strength). You may be able to improve your competitive position by simplifying the buying process - providing your customers one stop shopping. You have already established momentum and credibility with your installed accounts and it is far easier and cost effective to sell them additional products than it is to win new customers.

8. Technology – Build or Buy? This is a quandary for most companies, but is especially acute for technology companies. Acquiring technology through the acquisition of another company can be an excellent growth strategy for several reasons. First, the R&D costs are generally lower for these smaller, agile, more narrowly focused companies than their larger, higher overhead acquirers. Secondly, time to market, window of opportunity, first mover advantage can have a huge impact on the ultimate success of a product. It has been said that Alexander Graham Bell arrived four hours before another inventor at the patent office for essentially the same invention. If there is a good idea or a market opportunity, most likely it is being pursued independently and simultaneously on several fronts. First one to establish their product as the "standard" is the big winner. I sure would not want to try to displace Microsoft Windows as the operating system for PC's.

9. Acquisition to Provide Scale and Access to Capital Markets – In this area, bigger is better. Larger companies can generally weather a storm better than smaller companies and are considered safer investments. Larger companies command larger valuation multiples. Some companies make acquisitions in order to get big enough to attract public capital in the form of an IPO or investments from Private Equity Groups. Many smart business owners have consolidated several smaller companies at lower multiples to create a larger company that the investment community valued at higher multiples. This can be a very effective grow to exit strategy.

10. Protect and Expand Mature Product Lines - I recently came across an outstanding example of the execution of this strategy. Johnson & Johnson, the multi-billion dollar pharmaceutical company in 2000 acquired Alza Corporation, the maker of drug delivery systems and devices for what appeared to be an unbelievably steep price of $13.7 billion, or 23 times year 2000 revenues. They are the inventors of the transdermal patch used in products such as NicoDerm CQ. They have developed time released pills that can, for example deliver Ritalin, the drug for attention deficit disorder in children, at prescribed times with one dose. They have developed an injectable titanium stint to deliver cancer medication over the course of

a year. Why would J&J pay so much for this company? Here is the strategy. The latest price tag for getting a major new drug through the FDA and to market is a whopping $800 million. These delivery technologies can turn J&J's old drugs into new best sellers that are re-patentable at a far lower price than new drug development. An added benefit is that they can do the same for off patent drugs from other competitors.

11. Protect Customer Base from Competition – The telephone companies have done studies that show that with each additional product or service that a customer uses, the likelihood of the customer defecting to a competitor drops exponentially. In other words, get your customers to use local, long distance, cellular, cable, broadband, etc and you will not lose them. Multiple products and services provided to the same customer dramatically improve retention rates. At the risk of repeating myself, it costs ten times more to get a new customer than it does to keep one.

12. Acquisition to Remove Barriers to Entry – An example of execution of this strategy is a large commercial information technology consulting firm acquiring a technology consulting firm that specializes in the Federal Government. The larger IT Consulting firm had valuable expertise and best practices that were easily transferable to government business if they could only break the code of the vendor approval process. After many fits and starts to do it themselves, they simply acquired a firm that had an established presence. They were able to then bring their full capabilities from the commercial side to effectively increase their newly acquired government business.

13. Opportunistic Acquisition for when the Market Turns – as they taught me in business school: buy low and sell high. Well-run businesses often will buy competitors that bring many of the benefits from above at very favorable prices when times are tough. They buy customers, new geographies, technology, management talent, etc. at less than strategic prices because they have the staying power to last through a market downturn. Buying a company that doesn't fit at a bargain is ultimately not a bargain if you are unable to integrate to make your core business more powerful.

Larger firms with lots of resources have established business development offices to execute corporate growth strategies through acquisition. These experienced buyers search for companies that fit their well-defined acquisition criteria. In most cases they are attempting to buy companies that are not actively for sale. If a strategic company is for sale and is being represented by an M&A firm, the M&A firm's job is to sell that strategic value to the marketplace. If properly done, the buyers are competing with several other buyers that recognize the strategic value and the price tends to be bid way up. The win for the successful corporate acquirer is to target several candidates that have many of the characteristics from above, buy them at financial valuation multiples (traditional valuation techniques like discounted cash flow or EBITDA multiples), integrate to strength and achieve strategic performance.

CHAPTER 4

Planning For The Sale

4.1 – Business Owners Face An Asset Allocation Issue

If this recent market meltdown has taught us anything it is to make sure you are diversified over several investments and asset classes. Would your financial advisor recommend that you put 80% or more of your assets into a single investment? Of course not, but a large percentage of business owners actually have that level of concentration. On top of that, privately held businesses are illiquid assets often requiring one to two years to sell.

So for your baby boomer business owner, it is

time to recognize the importance of planning for your business exit or business sale. It is time to move your thinking about your business from - the vehicle to provide income to your family, and start thinking about it in terms of wealth maximization. Below is a graphical comparison between a business owner and another high net worth individual.

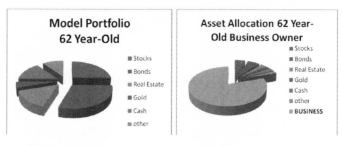

Business owners are typically not proactive when it comes to exit planning or succession planning in their business because it forces them to embrace their own mortality. If an owner has a sudden debilitating health issue or unexpectedly dies, instead of getting full value for the company, his estate can sell it out of bankruptcy two years later for ten cents on the dollar. This is a punishing financial result for the lack of appropriate planning.

There are many complex issues involved in a business transition or a business sale. Poor decisions at this critical time can result in swings of hundreds of thousands or even millions of dollars. If you can take away one thing from this, it would be to actively get out in front of the process with your professional advisors. This decision and how it is executed will be the single most impactful event in your family's financial future.

As business owners approach retirement, they often seek help with investment decisions that employ sound diversification and liquidity strategies. Your business is generally the largest, most illiquid, and most risky investment in your total wealth portfolio. Your successful business exit should be executed with the same diligence, knowledge, experience and skill that you have regularly applied to the organizing, running and building your business.

4.2 – THE TEN COMMANDMENTS OF SELLING MY BUSINESS

1. Thou shall not wait too long. Have you ever heard, "I sold my business to early?" Compare that with the number of times you've heard somebody say, "I should have sold my business two years ago." Unfortunately, waiting too long is probably the single biggest factor in reducing the proceeds from the sale of a privately held business. The erosion in business value typically is most pronounced in that last year before exiting. The decision to sell is often times a reactive decision rather than a proactive decision. An individual who spends 20 years running their business and controlling their outcomes often behaves differently in the exit from his business. The primary reasons for selling are events such as a serious health issue, owner burnout, the death of a principal, general industry decline, or the loss of a major customer. Exit your business from a position of strength, not from the necessity of weakness. Don't let that next big deal delay your sale. You can reward yourself for that transaction you project to close with an intelligently written sale agreement containing contingent payments in the future if that event occurs.

2. Thou shall to be prepared personally. We all create business plans both formally and informally. We all plan for vacations. We plan our parties. We need to plan for the most important financial event of our lives, the sale of our business. Typically a privately held business represents greater than 80% of the owner's net worth. Start out with your plans of how you want to enjoy the rewards of your labor.

Where do you want to travel? What hobbies have you been meaning to start? What volunteer work have you meant to do? Where do you want to live? What job would you do if money were not in issue? You need to mentally establish an identity for yourself outside of your business.

3. Thou shall prepare my business for sale. Now that you are all excited about the fun things you'll do once you exit your business, it's now time to focus on the things that you can do to maximize the value of your business upon sale. This topic is enough content for an entire article, however, we will briefly touch upon a couple of important points. First, engage a professional CPA firm to do your books. Buyers fear risk. Audited or reviewed financial statements from a reputable accounting firm reduced the perception of risk. Do not expect the buyer to give you credit for something that does not appear in your books. If you find that a large percentage of your business comes from a very few customers, embark on a program immediately to reduced customer concentration. Buyers fear that when the owner exits the major customers are at risk of leaving as well. Start to delegate management activities immediately and identify successors internally. If you have no one that fits that description and you have enough time, seek out, hire and train that individual that would stay on for the transition and beyond. Buyers want to keep key people that can continue the momentum of the business. Analyze and identify the growth opportunities that are available to your business. What new products could I introduced to our existing customer base? What new markets could utilize our products? What strategic alliances would help grow my business? Capture that in a document and identify the resources required to pursue this plan. Buyers will have their own plans, but you'll increase their perception of the value of your business through your grasp of the growth opportunities.

4. Thou shall keep my eye on the ball. A major mistake business owners make in exiting their business is to focus their time and attention on selling the business as opposed to running the business. This occurs in large publicly traded companies with deep management teams as well as in private companies where management is largely in the hands of a single individual. Many large companies that are in the throws of being acquired are guilty of losing focus on the day-to-day operations. In case after case these businesses suffer a significant competitive downturn. If the acquisition does not materialize, their business has suffered significant erosion in value. For a privately held business the impact is even more acute. There simply is not enough time for the owner to wear the many hats of operating his business while embarking on a full-time job of selling his business. The owner wants the impending sale to be totally confidential until the very last minute. If the owner attempts to sell the business himself, by default he has identified that his business is for sale. Competitors would love to have this information. Bankers get nervous. Employees get nervous. Customers get nervous. Suppliers get nervous. The owner has inadvertently created risk, a potential drop in business and a corresponding drop in the sale price of his business.

5. Thou shall get multiple buyers interested in my business. The "typical" business sale transaction for a privately held business begins with either an unsolicited approach by a competitor or with a decision on the part of the owner to exit. If a competitor initiates the process, he typically isn't interested in over paying for your business. In fact, just the opposite is true. He is trying to buy your business at a discount. Outside of yourself there is no one in a better position to understand the value of your business more than a major competitor. He will try to keep the sales process limited to a negotiation of one. In our mergers and acquisitions practice the owner often approaches us after an unsolicited offer. What we have found is generally that unsolicited buyer is not the ultimate purchaser, or if he is, the final purchase price is, on average 20% higher than the original offer. If the owner decides to exit and initiates the process, it usually begins with a communication with a trusted advisor – accountant, lawyer, banker, or financial advisor. Let's say that the owner is considering selling his business and he tells his banker. The well- meaning banker says, "One of my other customers is also in your industry. Why don't I provide you an introduction?" If the introduction results in a negotiation of one, it is unlikely that you will get the highest and best the market has to offer.

6. Thou shall hire a Mergers and Acquisitions firm to sell my business. You improve your odds of maximizing your proceeds while reducing the risk of business erosion by hiring a firm that specializes in selling businesses. A large public company would not even consider an M&A transaction without representation from a Merrill Lynch, Goldman Sachs, Solomon Brothers or other high profile investment banking firm. Why? With so much at stake, they know they will do better by paying the experts. Companies in the $3 Million to $50 Million range fall below their radar, but there are mid market M&A firms that can provide similar services and process. Generally when you sell your business, it is the one time in your life that you go through that experience. The buyer of the last company we represented for sale had previously purchased 25 companies. The sellers were good business people, knew their stuff, but this was their first and probably last business sale. Who had the advantage in this transaction? By engaging a professional M&A firm they helped balance the M&A experience scales.

7. Thou shall engage other professionals that have experience in business sale transactions. You may have a great outside accountant that has done your books for years. If he has not been involved in multiple business sales transactions, you should consider engaging a CPA firm that has the experience to advise you on important tax and accounting issues that can literally result in swings of hundreds of thousands of dollars. What are the tax implications of a stock purchase versus an asset purchase? A lower offer on a stock purchase may be far superior to a higher offer on an asset purchase after the impact of taxes on your realized proceeds. Is the accountant that does your books qualified to advise you on that issue? Would your accountant know the best way to allocate the purchase price on an asset sale between hard assets, good will, employment agreements and non-compete agreements? A deal attorney is very different from the attorney you engage for every day business law issues. Remember, each element of deal structure that is favorable to the seller for tax or risk purposes is generally correspondingly unfavorable to the buyer, and vice versa. Therefore the experienced team for the buyer is under instructions to make an offer with the most favorable tax and reps and warranties consequences for their client. You need a professional team that can match the buyer's team's level of experience with deal structure, legal, and tax issues.

8. Thou shall be reasonable in my expectations on sales price and terms. The days of irrational exuberance are over. Strategic buyers, private equity groups, corporate buyers, and other buyers are either very smart or do not last very long as buyers. I hate rules of thumb, but generally there is a range of sales prices for similar businesses with similar growth profiles and similar financial performance. That being said, however, there is still a range of selling prices. So, for example, let's say that the sales price for a business in the XYZ industry is a multiple of between 4 and 5.5 times EBITDA. Your objective and the objective of a good M&A advisor is to sell your business at the top end of the range under favorable terms. In order for you to sell your business outside of that range you must have a very compelling competitive advantage, collection of intellectual property, unusual growth prospects, or significant barriers to entry that would justify a premium purchase price. If you think about the process of detailing your car before you offer it for sale, a good M&A advisor will assist you in that process for your business. Let's say, for example, that 4 to 5.5 multiple from above was the metric in your industry and you had an EBITDA for the last fiscal year of $2.5 million. Your gross transaction proceeds could range from $10 million to $13.75 million. A skilled M&A firm with a proven process can move you to the top of your industry's range. The impact of hitting the top of the sales price range vs. the bottom more than justifies the success fee you pay to your M&A professionals.

9. Thou shall disclose, disclose, disclose, and do it early. A seemingly insignificant minor negative revealed early in the process is an inconvenience, a hurdle, or a point to negotiate around. That same negative revealed during negotiations, or worse yet, during due diligence, becomes, at best, a catalyst for reexamining the validity of every piece of data to, at worse, a deal breaker. No contract in the world can cover every eventuality if there is not a fundamental meeting of the minds and a trust between the two parties. Unless you are lucky enough to get an all cash offer without any reps and warranties, you are going to be partnered with your buyer for some period in the future. Buyers try to keep you on the hook with reps and warranties that last for a few years, employment contracts, or non-competes that last, escrow funds, seller notes, etc. These all serve a dual role to reduce the risk of future surprises. If future material surprises occur, buyers tend to be punitive in their resolution with the seller. Volunteer to reveal your company's warts early in the process. That will build trust and credibility and will ensure you get to keep all of the proceeds from your sale.

10. Thou shall be flexible and open to creative deal structure. Everything is a negotiation. You may have in mind that you want a gross purchase price of $13 million and all cash at close. Maybe the market does not support both targets. You may be able to get creative in order to reach that purchase price target by agreeing to carry a seller note. If the sale process produces multiple bids and the best one is $11.3 million cash at close. You may counter with a 7-year seller balloon note at 8% for $3 million with $10 million cash at close. If the buyer is a solid company, that may be a superior outcome than your original target because the best interest return you can currently get on your investments is 4%. Be flexible, be creative, and use your team to negotiate the hard parts and preserve your relationship with the buyer.

You may have spent your life's work building your business to provide you the income, wealth creation, and legacy that you had planned and hoped for. You prepared and were competitive and tireless in your approach. You have one final act in your business. Make that your final business success. Exit on purpose and do it from a position of strength and receive the highest and best deal the market has to offer.

4.3 – Ten Reasons to Sell Your Information Technology Company

For the past 20 years you have built your information technology business. Your company has become part of your identity. Even when you are not at work, you are working, thinking, planning. You never stop. If you sell you are leaving behind much more than a job. In this article we will discuss some reasons that might indicate that it is time to sell your information technology company.

1. Late in your working life you are faced with a major system re-write, sales force expansion or capital requirement in order for your company to maintain its competitive position.

2. A large competitor is taking market share away from you at an accelerating pace.

3. Your legacy system or competitive advantage has been "leap frogged" by a smaller, nimble, entrepreneurial firm.

4. A major company just acquired a direct competitor and will be aggressively growing the business.

5. Your fire to compete at your top level is not burning as brightly as it once did.

6. Your kids are not interested or are not capable of running the business.

7. You have had a health scare and have decided to smell the flowers.

8. You have lost a major client of a key employee.

9. The market is hot and you decide to take some chips off the table for asset diversification.

10. You exit in an orderly fashion and from a position of strength as you intended.

Lets look at these in a little more detail.

Major capital investment, system upgrade or sales force expansion required - You are supposed to be diversifying your assets, not concentrating them even further. Think about a simple payback analysis. Does that extend beyond your retirement date? You want to be able to defend that investment with the energy and intensity you devoted when you were originally growing your business. Maybe it is time to bring in an equity partner with smart money, an industry buyer with the management depth, infrastructure, or distribution network to protect that investment. You might consider selling now with a three-year employment contract. Let the new owner fund the required capital investment and defend that investment with his larger capital base.

A Large Competitor is Taking Market Share Away from You - Believe me, the news is not going to get better. As an investor you would probably sell the stock in a company you owned if Microsoft or GE decided to assume a presence in that market. Business owners often struggle with objectivity when a similar event takes place in their own company's industry.

Your Legacy Systems have been "Leap Frogged"

by a Nimble Entrepreneurial Firm - This happens all the time and can cause an erosion of your customer base. Your inertia will sustain you for a while, but eventually you will begin to experience customer defections. You can either rewrite, acquire or sell. If you decide to sell, do so before losing too many clients.

A giant company in your industry just acquired one of your major competitors. Watch out, they did not make this acquisition to maintain status quo. They want to grow their market share. They will be coming after your clients. The good news is that as a defensive measure, one or more of their competitors will be compelled to make a similar acquisition. It is best to be aggressively ahead of the curve and get acquired while the market is hot and prices are being bid upwards.

Your interest and competitive fire is eroding. Let's face it, if you are not growing, you most likely are contracting. Your competition was tough when you were on your game. Your family's net worth is under attack if you are no longer fully committed.

Your original plan was to turn your business over to your children. They may not be interested or capable of competing at this level. Perhaps the greatest legacy you can leave to your kids is to convert your company into a diversified portfolio of financial assets that are far less risky than turning complex company in a highly competitive industry over to inexperienced managers.

You have a health scare and all of a sudden you start thinking of all the sacrifices you made and all the things you want to do before it is too late. Your list of goals is immediately changed from financial in nature to family, friends, travel, experiences, philanthropy, etc. You might want to listen to your heart this time.

You have lost a major client or a key employee. That can be a real blow to a business. The owner, by nature, is optimistic and believes that the lost business will soon be replaced and does not ratchet down the expense level to match this new sales level. If he does cut, inevitably, it is not fast enough and not deep enough. Maybe it is time to seek a buyer that could replace that business before your company's value is severely impaired as your profits erode.

The market is hot and you decide to take some chips off the table for diversification. You may be thinking of retiring in four years, but a consolidation is occurring in your industry and valuations are up 20%. Sell at the top and sign a four-year employment or consulting contract. The odds are that if you exit on your original schedule, valuations will have settled back down to the norm.

You ring the bell and exit on your own terms, from a position of strength, exactly like you planned. You are well aware of the competitive forces in the market and the relative strength or weakness in valuation multiples. You have prepared your business to be attractive to a strategic buyer. Everything is going your way. You hire a good M&A advisory firm to present you confidentially to the most likely buyers. Several recognize your value and show interest. You are able to get a little competitive bidding going. Your transaction value rises and your terms improve. You pull the trigger and complete the sale. Mission Accomplished.

4.4 – Treat it Like an Investment

Think of the joy you feel when you look back and realize that you sold a stock at a big profit and got out within a few percentage points of its all time high. You chuckle a bit as you watch the stock pull back by over 100% while you have redeployed your proceeds into other diversified investments that have performed well. That is a very disciplined approach to investing and unfortunately I have failed to execute that on several very costly occasions.

So now I preach to business owners to execute the same dispassionate approach when it comes to their privately held business. It is so much more than an arm's length investment. It is their life's work, their identity, their pride and joy. The very nature of the entrepreneur means they are confident and optimistic, otherwise they would not have started the business in the first place. This attitude can really cost them in both good times and bad. When things are going well, he projects that they will get even better. When things go poorly, he reasons that this is just a short term issue and he will power through it.

Getting back to investing for a minute, I find that my best decisions are made when the market is closed and I am in planning mode. I might put on a stop loss order for that mining stock that has run up 40% in the last 3 months or put in a sell order if it hits 50% above its previous 52 week high. I might place a buy order for a hot stock anticipating a pull-back rather than buying it in a high volume upward move. I am trying to take the emotion out of my decision making by planning ahead for my trigger points.

For a business owner, it is important to recognize something is always for sale at the right price and terms. The business owner needs to recognize trigger points, both positive and negative and should establish a plan to be able to act upon them. Some positive triggers are you just had your most profitable year ever, you just got your first big order from the coveted blue chip account, or you just introduced a promising new product. The owner thinks this trend will continue indefinitely.

On the negative side, triggers might be your largest account runs into financial difficulty, the loss of a key employee, a health issue with the owner, or a competitor that has introduced an improvement on your major product. The owner believes that these are just challenges that he can manage his way around.

On the positive end, you can very effectively sell the trend to potential acquirers. Often times competitive forces act to bring the short term upward trend back closer to the norm. If the owner in his optimism waits to capture a second helping of his initial trend, he may have moved back to the norm and can no longer sell the positive trend.

If, on the other hand, an owner, especially later in his working life, tries to power through a negative trigger, the likelihood is that his business is in for a protracted downward slide. If he recognizes this in advance and has prepared for his exit, he may be able to sell the company before too much financial damage has occurred. A strong buyer can stop the slide if they get involved early enough. Just like you can sell the trend on the upside, the market will impose the negative trend on your company's selling price with a downward trend.

The Basics of Exit Preparation

1. Recognition of potential financial impact

• Your business is likely your family's largest asset. In many cases it represents over 80% of your family's net worth.

• Your business is illiquid and the price is subject to broad interpretation by the market.

• Your business can not be sold quickly. An orderly business sale usually takes between 6 and 12 months.

• If you have a debilitating health issue and are not able to work or you die, your business value could drop 20, 30, 40% or more over a very short period of time.

• Buyers will be predatory if you are selling from a position of weakness

2. Have your business in move in condition at all times

• Have a well-documented procedure manual

• Make sure that there is management in place (beside the owner) that has decision making ability and authority

• Create a growth plan – a 5 to 10 page document identifying the potential you have created in your business and where you would invest to grow if you had greater resources

• Have your books reviewed by an outside CPA

- Ensure your data processing systems are updated and reflect best practices in your industry

- Institutionalize your customers - they are owned by the company, not by the salesman

- Institutionalize your vendors

- Move whatever time and materials business and handshake business to contracts if possible

- Provide price incentives to move short term contracts to longer term contracts

Once you have acknowledged the importance of your exit strategy and put these disciplines in place, you can be prepared for the triggers that either you create or that have been created in the marketplace. An important point to recognize is that your business sale date will not necessarily be your retirement date. More often than not the new owner will want your continued involvement for some time after the sale.

So let's say that there is a positive trigger like a

big consolidation in your industry at very attractive multiples. You could sell now and stay on for one year or perhaps several more in a different or reduced role. You could wind down from the rigors or day-to-day management and take on the role of CEO – Chief Evangelical Officer.

4.5 – Groom or Hire Your Successor

One of the exciting aspects of being involved in Mergers and Acquisitions is that we are constantly learning. One of our most productive classrooms is the buyer visit. In those visits the buyer's motivations, priorities, concerns, and value drivers and value detractors are often revealed.

This was the case in one recent buyer visit with our client. Her Firm is representative of many early baby boomer led firms that "started the business in their garage" (actually it was started in her living room) 25 years ago and built a successful business with an excellent brand and customer loyalty. She is now looking to exit her business and reap the rewards from her hard work in the form of a generous buy-out offer.

The potential buyer is a business owner that started a similar firm at about the same time, but has morphed into part business owner and part private equity investor. He brings a unique perspective of analyzing this acquisition wearing two hats – one as a strategic industry buyer and the second as a disciplined financial buyer. It was quite instructive to watch the dual motivations at play during the visit.

While wearing his industry buyer hat, he was quite excited about the synergies of the two companies, the growth potential, and the new vertical market that the combined firm could capture. While wearing his private equity investor hat, however, that excitement was dampened by the risk that our owner had created with her company. The owner and her top producer directly touch 70% of the company's revenues. They are the face of the company. They are the "brand". They are also in retirement mind set and have not groomed a capable successor internally.

Even though we have coached our clients with the "We will stay on for a period of time to transition our relationships and transfer the intellectual capital" speech, the buyer perceives huge risk. Quite frankly, I completely agree with his thinking. As this issue was explored, it became evident that this factor would negatively impact both the transaction value and the deal structure. Translation – a discounted purchase price and much of that price deferred in the form of a multi-year earn out payment.

The good news was the buyer's strategic side recognized the value of the new vertical market our client's company would allow him to enter in full stride. He also recognized, because our client was represented by an investment banker, that there will be other buyers competing for this prize. The buyer came up with a very creative approach. Because this new vertical market is so strategic to him and recognizing the lack of management depth in the target company, he had initiated discussions with two individuals that were high caliber executives from the new vertical.

The buyer laid out his plan to our clients and asked permission to introduce this potential acquisition to the two candidates as a simultaneous acquisition and hiring scenario. Our client is very concerned about confidentiality and pushed back. The buyer then countered with two purchase platforms – one with the new hire as successor and one without. The one with the new hire was far superior in terms of both total transaction value and in the percentage of that value that would be paid at closing versus paid as and earn out.

After some discussion with our client and a review of the financial implications, we agreed to the buyer's plan to introduce this opportunity to his two candidates with the execution by them of a confidentiality agreement.

This dramatic contrast in transaction value and terms really helped quantify and crystallize what we have intuitively known for many years. To use the words of Curley from The Three Stooges, "If you want to catch a mouse, you have to think like a mouse." Our translation is, "If you want to sell your company for maximum value, you have to think like a buyer."

The lack of an internal successor, the lack of management depth, the concentration of account relationships and intellectual capital into one or two key people that are likely to leave shortly after a transaction will result in at best, huge discounts in your company selling price and at worst, will make your company a non-viable acquisition target.

Contrast this current situation to a client that we represented a few years back and you will understand our advice. The previous owner client recognized that he was going to sell his company two years prior to the event. He started grooming an internal successor, giving up most of his own direct involvement. When he was satisfied that this transition was operating smoothly, he fired himself as president and promoted his protegee into that position. He allowed the company to operate successfully in this mode for one year and then engaged us to sell his company. The results were as planned – no worries about post transaction client or employee defections and no discounts on the business selling price.

Our advice to business sellers is to begin your business exit process well in advance of your exit. Give up your natural tendency to be involved in every aspect of your business. Relinquish control, delegate, develop your staff. Promote your successor into day-to-day responsibility. If you do not have a capable internal candidate, go out and hire one. Your added expense will be more than offset and rewarded with a much higher business selling price.

4.6 – Passing The Business To The Next Generation – Is It Best For Your Family?

Although it is a noble gesture, passing a business down to the next generation is more often than not, unsuccessful. In fact, statistics show that only one-third of all family businesses are successfully transferred to the next generation and only 13% are transferred onto the third generation.

Many family business consultants say the primary reason for this low survival rate is the failure to develop and effectively plan for the transfer of ownership and management of the closely held family business. I agree that this is a factor, but in my dealing with family businesses I find that there are some more fundamental reasons. The first is that the next generation has a lot different life style than the business founder and entrepreneur. They do not share the same drive and commitment that dad needed to build the business from scratch. They go to the good schools, get a taste of the good life and generally do not share the passion of the business founder. I recently was involved in selling a produce distributor. I found that most of the firms were in their second or third generation. I asked a third generation owner why this particular industry had such success with keeping the business in the family. He said, "When you are up and on the docks at 3 am and work 12 hour days, you don't have the time to spend the money."

The next generation may have a grand scheme to turn the traditional printing business into a media empire or a liquor business into an entertainment enterprise. A few years back the second generation of a well known Chicago area computer leasing and IT Services Firm tried to turn it into an Internet Venture Firm with disastrous results.

Before you just assume that your torch will be carried by the next generation, make sure that the next generation even wants to run the business. Imagine the loss in value that would have occurred if the real estate billionaire from the western suburbs had turned his empire over to his son who simply wanted to produce plays.

Are your heirs even capable of running your business? Have you held on to the reins so tightly that the kids involved in the business have not been able to develop their decision-making or leadership skills? Do they command company respect because of their personal strength and skills or are they grudgingly granted respect because they are the child of the owner? If that is the case, the odds are not good for them taking over when you retire.

Another big challenge is trying to balance fairness in employing many children or even grandchildren in a family business with various skill levels, compensation levels and ownership levels. The jealousy and in fighting can absolutely grind the company's progress to a halt.

The business owner must make some difficult decisions when he or she decides it is time for them to retire. Why did I create this business? Was it to keep this business in the family for generations or was it to provide for my family for generations? If the desire and the capability of the children are not evident and the company is large enough, it may be the right decision to first get outside board members actively involved as step one. Step two would be to hire professional management to run the business. A second alternative is to sell the company while you are still running it and it can command its highest value. If you have children that want to remain in the business for the immediate future, incorporate that into the sale agreement with employment contracts.

Another way to think of it is, while I am running the business, the best ROI is to keep the bulk of my net worth invested in this company. If I am no longer running the company what is the best risk reward profile for my net worth? Would my heirs be better off if the business was sold and the value converted to financial assets?

4.7 – Strategic Value - Asset Inventory Checklist

Instructions: Review this list and identify any of these factors that a larger industry buyer would be able to leverage to grow revenues after they have acquired your company. For example: Computer Database – OUR COMPANY has a database of 2,000 current and former customers with complete contact information including email address. We also have a prospect database of over 20,000 potential clients. Now copy this ASSET INVENTORY CHECKLIST into a Word document, check ones that apply, write a brief description of your company's strategic asset to replace the description provided in the CHECKLIST. As you build your business for your eventual exit, focus on further developing the assets you already have and nurture the development of others that may be relevant to your business.

Advertising campaign - A proven campaign that is effective in driving additional business

Advertising materials - Fully developed

advertising messaging and collateral materials

Assignable contracts - A clause in customer contracts that allows transfer upon change in ownership

Backlog - Self explanatory. Wouldn't we all like to have Boeing's 7 year backlog?

Barriers to entry - Takes on many forms from difficult regulatory environment, to licenses and permits, to complexity of technology and many more

Blue Chip Customers - Very valuable and difficult to obtain in a competitive market

Branding - Ask Coke, Apple, McDonalds - same status in your industry niche

Computer database - You have digitized your company's assets - customers, personnel, prospects, procedures, trade secrets, manuals, etc.

Computer designs - CAD CAM and other engineering digital assets

Copyrights - Depending on your industry can be hugely valuable

Cost to duplicate your technology - Whether it is software, a biologic medicine, a specialized process, etc, it would be far cheaper and faster to buy than develop

Credit files - Industry specific value.

Custom-built factory - Competitive advantage for keeping down cost of production

Delivery systems - Not just limited to Logistics providers.

Distributorship - A well developed distribution channel is highly scalable

Employee manual - Valuable from a cultural asset to liability protection

Employee turnover - A low level of turnover indicates a very attractive work environment. Turnover is very expensive.

Employee on-boarding process - Think Zappos - the process promotes long term employee retention

Experienced design staff - History of product success very difficult to duplicate or replace

Favorable financing - Proven banking relationships provide more options and flexibility

Franchises - Successful business model for efficient rapid growth

Government programs - Getting approval is difficult and time consuming - barrier to entry

Growing industry - Natural enhancer to company growth rate and improved valuation multiple

High cost to acquire customers - If it requires long sales cycle and skilled salesmen, your install base has high value because it cost dearly to obtain

Integrated CRM system - Not just having one, but implementing industry best practices around populating it and leveraging it to drive and support business

Key employee agreements - Benefit everything from retention, to IP protection, to non-compete

Know-how - What is your company's specialized knowledge that gives you a competitive advantage? Sales system, technology, value proposition, subject matter expert

Licenses/Permits - From land fill permits to a grandfathered liquor license, whatever approvals that are difficult to obtain provide barriers to entry

Limited customer concentration - No customer accounting for more than 5% of total business reduces your risk and the risk of a potential buyer

Local economy - The trend is your friend. A thriving local economy is good for business

Location - Whether it is a prime corner in retail or availability of skilled workers, location can be a big advantage

Long-term contracts - Huge value in predictability of revenues and very important risk reduction for a potential business buyer

Loyal customer base - Stability of earnings and fertile ground for new product offerings

Mailing list (email list) - Valuable source of new business

Management - Highly valued for contribution to current owner's business and highly coveted for a potential buyer of the business

Multi-channel distribution - Reduces the risk of customer defections from nimble competitors with minimum overhead

Name recognition - See Branding

New markets (industries) - Can your current products be positioned to appeal to new industries

New markets (geography) - Can your current products be distributed t to new geographic markets

Outbound sales system - Expensive to implement and maintain. Most are under performing

Patents - Sometimes the value for a smaller company is your willingness to defend them. For a large company buyer they are highly valued

Pricing power with new owner - Very subtle, but highly strategic and valuable. In the market you discount to compete against brand player. If you are acquired by brand player, they can raise prices across the board

Proprietary designs - IP not necessarily on balance sheet but important competitive differentiator

Published articles - Viewed as subject matter expert, industry status, invited speaker at industry events, great "free" marketing resource

Recession-resistant industry - Highly valued by financial buyers as well as strategic buyers with a portfolio of cyclical properties

Recurring revenue model - The magic business model. Most software companies are converting to this model as SaaS. Reduces risk and smoothes out revenues

Regulatory advantage Give me an edge. Railroads, pipelines, landfills, what is yours?

Reputation - With big companies it is brand, small companies it is reputation - very valuable no matter what you call it

Royalty agreements - Ask the song writers, actors, drug discoverers what they think about this as a business model. Even more magical than recurring revenue model. Here you produce once and it returns over and over

Scalable business model - Very important for a small business owner whose limitations are risk tolerance and access to capital. A strategic buyer will recognize this potential

Security clearances - Very important for government contracts and security work. These alone can make your company by a large company looking for those clearances.

Skilled employees - Hard to get, motivate and retain. If your company has them, the strategic buyers see their value.

Social media momentum - For the uninitiated, this is a significant investment on the front end. Once established, it is a highly scalable business advantage

Strong referenceable accounts - No better source of new business than good old fashion referrals

Supplier base - A valuable asset of familiarity, trust, and execution

System & procedures - Technology is not the only area of innovation. Better management systems, executive dash boards, agile development are value drivers

Technology - Take your pick of industry, superior technology properly managed results in company competitive advantage

Thought leadership - Whether speaking, publishing or being interviewed, this carries the halo of business excellence and provides valuable company vibe

<u>Time to market advantage -</u> Very subtle but important strategic value driver. What do you have operational that a big company could duplicate in two years? How much business do they lose while in development?

<u>Tooling -</u> Big investment may be completely depreciated on the balance sheet, but the reality is it is more valuable than its original cost

<u>Trademarks -</u> Valuable to the extent that you leverage them to either drive business or fend off competition. May have greater value to large company buyer.

<u>Trade secrets -</u> Your company's special sauce. You know what it means to you. Now think how a deep pockets company buyer could leverage it.

<u>Training procedures -</u> Legendary at Xerox and IBM. On a smaller scale it can make your team a top performer. A buying company could learn from you.

4.8 – Market Timing is Critical

When a large software company makes an acquisition in a particular niche, several other comparable acquisitions soon follow. Let's explore this market dynamic and the importance for owners of similar software companies to reevaluate their exit plans.

Our firm was engaged as a merger and acquisition advisor in 2007 to sell a Content / Document Management Software Firm. We put together a database of likely buyers in that software category and began our contact process. Fast Forward to early 2010. We have been engaged by a second Content / Document Management Firm to sell their software company. From our earlier engagement, we dusted off our database of mid-market software companies in that space and began making our phone calls.

A very interesting thing happened. 40% of these middle market software companies had been acquired by one of the large software companies. We would call one document management software company expecting the receptionist to answer by the company name in our database. Instead, we got, "Thank you for calling OpenText." Next call, instead of the expected company name, we got an EMC Company. Another call and this time, "thank you for calling Oracle." Two calls later, we reach an IBM Company.

Wow. Between mid 2007 and early 2010, there was a buying spree by the enterprise software vendors shoring up their product offering to become a much more comprehensive offering, now called ECM or enterprise content management. It was almost like a heavyweight fight - IBM punches, EMC counters, and Oracle lands a blow while OpenText dodges a punch.

For the midsized software companies in this space, these were exciting times. This rapid consolidation and active buying caused the transaction values to increase rapidly. Once the enterprise companies have added what they needed, however, the buying stops, the market returns to normal and sellers no longer command a premium price.

Now the bad news. If you were a mid-sized competitor of the acquired companies, you are now competing with very large, powerful competitors. They will dwarf your company in terms of sales force size, marketing resources, brand awareness and pricing power. Their product now becomes the safe choice in a head-to -head competition with yours.

To now compete effectively will require even more skill. Your firm can continue to provide outstanding service and responsiveness. You can provide the small company customer attention that many customers require. You can be nimble and innovate with new products and features as another way to successfully compete.

You often hear the stock market pundits say, "the trend is your friend" or "don't fight the trend." There is a certain wisdom to this sentiment. If you are in a software category that suddenly has become the target for the big software vendors, you may do best to exit according to the market conditions rather than your original retirement schedule.

Actually, the buying company will most likely want you to stay on board for a period of time to transfer customer relationships and intellectual property. So you can take your chips off the table today at an opportune time for rich valuation multiples and then retire a few years later.

If you are younger, you can secure your family's financial future, work for the new company for a few years, gain valuable experience and then exit. Now you are ready to launch your next great idea.

This time it will be far easier. You will have a large base of resources and influential contacts. Also the venture capital guys might even give you money under reasonable terms. Home Run, touch em all!

4.9 – Buyers and Investors In Pre - Revenue Companies are an Endangered Species

Before you dismiss my premise and label me as one who is out of step with the highly publicized social media mega deals, I am excluding them from my population. I am excluding them because they have a very important characteristic of value and that is broad customer acceptance. That acceptance was generally accomplished virally and very inexpensively. The owner of that technology will, the wisdom goes, eventually figure out a way to monetize all of those valuable users.

For purposes of this analysis, I am limiting my population to technology based products and businesses that are aimed at the B2B marketplace. A good example might be application software. I may need a little help from Charles Darwin here with his theory of natural selection or may borrow from the saying that there are old pilots and there are bold pilots but very few old bold pilots.

Technology companies that buy other companies or professional investors that buy technology based companies generally have a first gate that all acquisitions have to pass in order to be considered as an acquisition candidate. Those targets must have real paying customers producing revenues, not necessarily profits, but that also is an often used helpful gate.

Another gate is the level of revenues. We have small software companies approach us and say that Microsoft or Google or Apple should buy them. They have $5 million in revenue. Unless they are in the massive user base category or have a quantum leap technology, there is no chance. The corporate development people in those organizations are under instructions to only consider move the needle opportunities. It takes as much resource to complete a $300 million acquisition as it does a $5 million acquisition. Where do you think these giants are focusing their resources?

In working with entrepreneurs we see several recurring themes. They are wonderfully optimistic. With the odds of succeeding in a start-up business not in their favor they must employ emotional blinders in order to press on. They believe their product compares very favorably on a feature/functionality basis with the leading competitive solutions on the market. Their estimate of both the TAM (total addressable market) and their eventual share of that market are highly aggressive. They under estimate the difficulty of reaching a critical mass of paying customers. And most importantly, they believe in their mission and deliver their message with the passion and commitment of a Billy Graham sermon.

We know from first-hand experience having represented several of these promising companies over the years. With this arsenal of optimism, these entrepreneurs have been pitching the corporate development departments, angel investors, venture capital funds, individual investors, friends and family, etc. You know what the buyers and investors all found out (even the super stars from Silicon Valley fail on 8 out of 10) was that they were not particularly good at picking the winners pre-revenue or pre- critical mass revenue.

Getting back to my Charles Darwin reference, the survivors evolved. They developed a characteristic that has enabled them to prosper. They no longer try to predict the winners pre-revenue. They let the market do it for them. No guru, no survey, no analytics is ever going to match the predictive power of the wisdom of crowds casting their economic vote to identify the winner.

The second gate, the size of revenue also performs a very important function especially when it comes to information technology or emerging technology. A large company will often expend as much internal resource in integrating a new product into their organization and rolling it out to their sales channel as they originally spent for the company acquisition. Given that backdrop, they want to eliminate or reduce as much as possible, the technology risk. In other words, does the stuff work and will it stand up to the rigors of thousands of users. A product that has achieved a critical mass of users has been subjected to the quality control of paying and renewing customers with other choices. The major bugs have been worked out and the product has gone through a continual feedback loop of improvement.

The company buyers/investors survivors recognized that it was too difficult to predict the winners pre-revenue, even with the smartest guys in the room, without a natural market vetting process. The economic vote of a critical mass of customers has proven to be the best of all predictors of success. When a technology entrepreneur hits this gate with his targeted buyer and gets quickly dismissed, it doesn't mean that he has a bad product, it means that he has one more step to take before the money starts to flow. Focus your resources on generating sales.

4.10 — Is Venture Capital Right for You?

I tried and I gave up. When we started out high-tech Merger and Acquisition Practice, I thought it a natural fit to also offer finder services for Entrepreneurs seeking Venture Capital Funding. That service is no longer available. Why not you ask? We failed miserably. Our firm has successfully completed several small high tech M&A deals at great multiples, but finding venture capital turned out to be a very frustrating and unproductive experience.

Unfortunately many high tech entrepreneurs have eventually landed on our doorstep totally drained from their experience of trying to raise venture funding themselves. Quite frankly, the process has caused several of these businesses to fail. According to venture industry statistics only 2% - 3% of firms seeking venture capital actually are successful in receiving funding. Only 2 out of 10 of those firms that receive funding provide the target returns for the Venture Firms. Since their failure rate is so high, they are looking for a 30 to 1 return on their money in their three or four year exit period.

It is generally not a good idea to alienate my readers, but the biggest problem that entrepreneurs have is that they are naïve about this whole process. They generally have unbridled optimism about the value of their company, idea, product, or technology in the marketplace. These entrepreneurs are usually the inventor or the author of the computer code and are not sales or business development guys.

They do not understand the sales process. After all, raising Venture Capital is the ultimate sales job. These tech-focused individuals will be strung along by the Venture firms unless they have a track record of starting a company and making investors rich. In that case the Venture Firms fight for their place in line to give you money. I would often speak with high-tech entrepreneurs who just completed "a great meeting" with XYZ Ventures. They would excitedly tell me that XYZ asked them for a report on this, pro-forma's for that, projections for this, a competitive analysis of the major players, etc. They would then schedule another meeting.

Our entrepreneur is thinking they are on the verge of landing the big one. My response is, "How much are they paying you for educating them on your space." The image that comes to mind is when you were a kid and were using a magnifying glass to burn up ants on an ant hill – kind of sadistic torture.

For you tech guys out there, this is not Field of Dreams – If you build it they will come. It is business and the mantra is – If you sell it they will come. Get over your bias of not valuing the sales process and go tap the best available sales and marketing person you can find to partner with you. Build a customer following that demonstrates a trend rather than a couple of isolated successes. Then go find a large strategic partner to acquire you at fantastic multiples. Work through your non-compete period and then launch your next great idea. Go to the venture guys from your new-found position of strength and tell them to get in the queue.

4.11 – Raising Venture Capital - Let's Be Realistic

I do not mean to discourage you entrepreneurs in your quest to launch the next Big Thing. Many of you look at your path as write a compelling business plan, make a few presentations to the well-known venture firms, get $3 million for 5% of your company pre revenue, and launch. Product development progresses without a hitch, you hit all of your milestones, you get a second round at an even more favorable valuation, and you land the big high-profile account. Two years later, you do an IPO with a market cap of $350 million. Fast forward another two years and you are the subject of a bidding war between Microsoft, Google, and Interactive Corp. You finally agree to a buy-out at $3 billion. Life is good.

Wow, that was easy. Unfortunately that is one in 10 million. I was listening to CNBC this morning and they were reporting on a new test developed by a Stanford PHD that would identify people two to six years in advance of developing Alzheimer's Disease. This is an ideal venture play - huge potential market, company founder with great credibility, and a great way to reduce future health care costs. On the surface this would seem like the sure fire bet for the venture guys, but the CNBC reporter said they were having trouble raising venture capital. What a shock.

If this company is having trouble, think about

the battle you face. Because no one has a crystal ball, seven out of ten venture investments totally fail. With that backdrop, venture capital investors look to achieve a thirty times return on their investment in three years. Many potentially successful companies fail to achieve the promise of their great idea because they get caught up in the venture trap. They are passionate about their idea and believe that it will become the next big success story. They tend to be very optimistic which is essential for one that takes the kind of risks that a start-up requires. Their biggest flaw is that they focus way too much of their efforts on the venture dance. Endless meetings and presentations followed by delays and more presentations to other members of the same venture teams.

There are other alternatives. How about a strategic alliance with a bigger company in your industry? What about a licensing deal with a big player? Can a value added reseller play a role for you? What about an outsourced sales effort? Should you sell your company? If you do have a great idea and are meeting an important market need, it is likely that there are other companies out there that have the same or very similar solutions. In today's business environment that translates into a very limited window of opportunity to achieve scale. You are on the clock to achieve scale before your funds run out or before a well funded competitor simply captures your market.

Venture is very glamorous, but do not be myopic in your approach to cashing out on your big idea. There are several very important alternatives including building a solid, profitable small company under the radar and then raising venture to achieve scale and take it to the next level.

4.12 – Clean Up Your Financials Well in Advance of Your Business Sale

When you sell your business, many factors are important in maximizing your selling price. Rock solid financials are job one before you sell. Here we discuss why you should remove all personal expenses from your business financials well in advance and how you will be rewarded in your business selling price.

Buying a business is a risky proposition. The buyer is attempting to examine and access all of the risk factors to determine how much to pay, what deal structure to propose, and even whether or not to even make an offer. What if I lose a key customer, employee, or supplier? What if our technology is surpassed by a new, lower-cost solution? What happens if a big company decides to enter our niche? These are just a few of the concerns that make buyers less generous in their offer price and terms. If your financials are questionable, that may be the deciding factor that diminishes your selling price or even blows up the deal.

Audited financials are the best to put a buyer's mind at ease. For smaller companies, the cost of this is not warranted. The next best are reviewed financials. They show that a CPA has put your accounting process through some review and scrutiny. Compiled statements are OK, but are closer to a book keeper's role than a CPA's approach. Just remember, the buyer's accountant is going to perform due diligence on your financials at a level closer to an audited statements process. If he finds mistakes and inconsistencies, a lack of trust on all other data can develop.

Your business tax returns will be gospel to the buyer because the IRS frowns on companies not reporting a portion of their income and that is what the buyer's bank reviews to determine the financing available for the acquisition.

In the Mergers and Acquisitions business we all

rely on "recast" financials to basically remove all of the expenses the owner runs through his business and make the company look more profitable to drive up the selling price. Sophisticated buyers (i.e. acquisition oriented corporations) may not directly confront you on the recasting, but they are not likely to give you full credit in their analysis. They may even develop some reservations about your character and ethics if the amounts are excessive. They may question your ability to fit in as a good corporate citizen as you transition your business to their institutional corporate structure.

If you are planning on selling your company in three years, why not start eliminating the expenses you run through the business that push the boundaries of business versus personal expenses? In the first year eliminate 33% of the country club, entertainment, business trips, conferences and non-contributing relatives on the payroll. The second year, eliminate another 33% of those and in the year preceding the sale, eliminate them completely.

Imagine the style points you would get from a sophisticated buyer when they discovered that your financials are really your financials with no recasting. Not only that, but you will likely receive a high end purchase price multiple and a greater percentage of cash at close. So, for example, if companies in your industry sell for a range of between 5 and 6.25 X EBITDA, then your company would likely sell at a multiple closer to the 6.25 high end than the 5 low end multiple.

If you had run $200,000 of owner expenses through the business and eliminated that practice you would pay approximately $80,000 in additional taxes. Your recast EBITDA would be higher than your reported EBITDA, but the sophisticated investor might only give you $100,000 credit and would adjust your multiple to the low end. Your recast EBITDA, for example, of $3.2 million would be credited by the buyer at $3.1 million with a valuation multiple of 5 X, resulting in a proposed purchase value of $15.5 million.

Compare this to using your real EBITDA of $3 million, but because it is not recast, your buyer pays a risk reduction premium in valuation multiple and moves you up to 6 X, resulting in a proposed purchase value of $18 million. This is a pretty impressive improvement in selling price for increasing your company's taxable income phased in over the three years prior to your business sale.

You may be asking yourself skeptically, how can this be? Remember, buying a business is all about minimizing the buyer's perception of risk. Now your financials are rock solid and do not require a long explanation on why they are really better than reported to the IRS. This is the most powerful risk reduction strategy available to business sellers. You will differentiate your company from every other acquisition target the buyer has reviewed. You increase your credibility on every other piece of information that you have provided during the courting and due diligence process. Their opinion on your business acumen, management ability, judgment, and ethics has been elevated. The buyer feels more confident that this will be a successful acquisition. For that they will pay a premium.

4.13 – Beware of the C Corp Asset Sale

We recently completed a Merger and Acquisition engagement to sell our client to a large publicly traded company. Our client had started her company 25 years ago and had set it up as a C Corp. She never was advised to change that structure in preparation for a much better tax treatment on the sale of the business.

The buyer had an acquisition policy of only asset sales and no stock sales. The tax implications to our client were punishing. In a C Corp Asset Sale, there is no such thing as a long-term capital gain for the corporation. Since our client's basis (a software and consulting firm) was essentially $0, the entire sale amount would have been treated as ordinary income and would have been taxed at a rate of about 30%. Once taxes are paid by the corporation and a distribution is made to the stockholders, the stockholders are then taxed at the 15% individual long-term capital gains rate.

Let's say that the purchase price was $5 million. With an asset sale, the Corporation would first pay 30% of $5 million, or $1.5 million. On the distribution, the shareholders would pay 15% of the $3.5 million distribution or $425,000. The total tax paid is a whopping $1,925,000. Net proceeds to the seller are $3,075,000. A stock sale, on the other hand is far superior for this C Corp. A stock sale is not taxed at the corporate level, so the gain of $5 million is taxed only once at the shareholders' long term capital gain tax rate of 15%, for a total tax of $750,000. Net proceeds to the seller are $4,250,000, an improvement of $1,175,000.

We simply had to turn this into a stock sale. Our approach was to use this issue as a negotiating point to bridge the valuation gap. The seller wanted more and the buyer wanted to pay less. We had pushed the value as far as could with the buyer, but our client still wanted more. We suggested to the buyer that if they were willing to do a stock sale we may be able to get our client to accept their current offer.

We argued that since this was a technology and services firm, the risk of any environmental or product liability was minimal. We proposed that they cover any perceived risks with stringent Reps and Warranties language in the purchase agreement. Finally, because a significant portion of the transaction value was an earn out, they had a built in escrow account. It worked! Our client was able to realize an additional $1,175,000 through a stock sale and we were able to bridge the valuation gap between buyer and seller.

CHAPTER 5

Seller Mistakes Destroy Value

5.1 – Ten Mistakes That Destroy Value

Selling your Software Company is the most important transaction you will ever make. Mistakes in this process can greatly erode your transaction proceeds. Do not spend twenty years of your toil and skill building your business like a pro only to exit like an amateur. Below are ten common mistakes to avoid:

1. Selling because of an unsolicited offer to buy – One of the most common reasons owners tell us they sold their business was they got an offer from a competitor or more often these days, an

Indian company looking to buy a customer base in the United States. If you previously were not considering this business sale, you probably have not taken some important personal and business steps to exit on your terms. The business may have some easily correctable issues that could detract from its value. You may not have prepared for an identity and lifestyle to replace the void caused by the separation from your company. If you are prepared, you are more likely to exit on your own terms.

2. Poor books and records – Business owners wear many hats. Sometimes they become so focused on the next version release that they are lax in financial record keeping. A buyer is going to do a comprehensive look into your financial records. If they are done poorly, the buyer loses confidence in what he is buying and his perception of risk increases. If he finds some negative surprises late in the process, the purchase price adjustments can be harsh. The transaction value is often attacked well beyond the economic impact of the surprise. Get a good accountant to do your books.

3. Going it alone – The business owner may be the foremost expert in GUI interfaces, but it is likely that his business sale will be a once in a lifetime occurrence. Mistakes at this juncture have a huge impact. It is especially critical to have a good M&A advisor if you are selling a software company because these companies do not fit traditional company valuation metrics. If an owner does not get the right representation and have several qualified buyers that covet his technology, he possibly can leave a lot of money on the table. Selling a software company is complex. Is it a better deal to structure some of the transaction value as an earn out based on post acquisition sales performance? Do you understand the difference in after tax proceeds between an asset sale and a stock sale? Your everyday bookkeeper may not, but a tax accountant surely does. Is your business attorney familiar with business sales legal work? Would he advise you properly on Reps and Warranties that will be in the purchase agreement? Your buyer's team will have this experience. Your team should match that experience of it will cost you way more than their fees.

4. Skeletons in the closet - If your company has any, the due diligence process will surely reveal them. One of the key issues in software companies is the clear title to intellectual property. Are your employee agreements well written? If you hired outside programmers, was their agreement specific in ownership of their output? The concern of the buyer is that once it becomes public that the deep pockets company is owner, previous disgruntled employees or contractors may resurface looking to bring legal action. Before your firm is turned inside out and the buyer spends thousands in this process and before the other interested buyers are put on hold – reveal that problem up-front. We sold a company that had an outstanding CFO. In the first meeting with us, he told us of his company's under funded pension liability. We were able to bring the appropriate legal and actuarial resources to the table and give the buyer and his advisors plenty of notice to get their arms around the issue. If this had come up late in the process, the buyer might have blown up the deal or attacked transaction value for an amount far in excess of the potential liability.

5. Letting the word out - Confidentiality in the business sale process is crucial. If your competitors find out, they can cause a lot of damage to your customers and prospects. It can be a big drain on employee morale and productivity. What if your head of systems development gets skittish and entertains offers from other companies and leaves while you are selling? The buyer wants your top people and they represent a significant portion of your future transaction value. If word you are for sale gets out, your suppliers and bankers get nervous. Nothing good happens when the work gets out that your company is for sale.

6. Poor Contracts – Here we mean the day-to-day contracts that are in place with employees, customers, contractors, and suppliers. Do your employees have non-competes, for example? If your company has intellectual property, do you have very clear ownership rights defined in your employee and contractor agreements. If not, you could be looking at meaningful escrow holdbacks post closing. Are your customer agreements assignable without consent? If they are not, customers could cancel post transaction. Your buyer will make you pay for this one way or another. If you are tempted to sign that big deal at bargain rates to pump up your business selling price, think again. Locking in a contract at below market rates could actually cause a discount to your selling price.

7. Bad employee behavior – You need to make sure you have agreements in place so that employees cannot hold you hostage on a pending transaction.

Key employees are key to transaction value. If you suspect there are issues, you may want to implement stay on bonuses. If you have a bad actor, firing him or her during a transaction could cause issues. You may want to be pre-emptive with your buyer and minimize any damage your employee might cause.

8. No understanding of your company's value – Business valuations are complex. A good business broker or M & A advisor that has experience in the software industry is your best bet. Business valuation firms are great for business valuations for gift and estate tax situations, divorce, etc. They tend to be very conservative and their results could vary significantly from your results from three strategic buyers in a battle to acquire your firm. Where a services business may sell for between 75% and 100% of last years sales, for example, software companies are all over the map. One of our clients had a coveted piece of software technology and was able to get 8 X last year's sales as his purchase price. We certainly could not have and would not have predicted that at the start of the engagement, but what a nice surprise. When it comes to selling your company, let the competitive market provide a value.

9. Getting into an auction of one – This is a silly visual, but imagine a big auction hall at Sotheby's occupied by an auctioneer and one guy with an auction paddle. "Do I hear $5 million? Anybody $5.5 million?" The guy is sitting on his paddle. Pretty silly, right? And yet we hear countless stories about a competitor coming in with an unsolicited offer and after a little light negotiating the owner sells. Another common story is the owner tells his banker, lawyer, or accountant that he is considering selling. His well-meaning professional says, "I have another client that is a software company. I will introduce you." The next thing you know the business is sold. Believe me, these folks are buying you business at a big discount. That's not silly at all!

10. Giving away value in negotiations and due diligence – When selling your business, your objective is to get the best terms and conditions. I know this is a shocker, but the buyer is trying to pay as little as possible and he is trying to get contractual terms favorable to him. These goals are not compatible with yours. The buyer is going to fight hard on issues like total price, cash at close, earn outs, seller notes, reps and warranties, escrow and holdbacks, post closing adjustments, etc. If you get into a meet in the middle compromise negotiation, before you know it, your Big Mac is a Junior Cheeseburger. Due diligence has a dual purpose. The first is obviously to insure that the buyer knows exactly what he is paying for. The second is to attack transaction value with adjustments. Of course this happens after their LOI has sent the other bidders away for 30 to 60 days of exclusivity. If you don't have a good team of advisors, this can get expensive

As my dad used to say, there is no replacement for experience. Another saying is that when a man with money and no experience meets a man with experience, the man with the experience walks away with the money and the man with the money walks away with some experience. Keep this in mind when contemplating the sale of your software company. It will likely be your first and only experience. Avoid these mistakes and make that experience a profitable one.

5.2 – A Single Buyer is a Prescription for Failure

Many business owners get approached by a single buyer with an unsolicited offer to buy the business. We will identify the pitfalls of entertaining this single buyer and what to do to improve your odds of getting a fair outcome.

When dealing with only one buyer, he is right. When there are multiple suitors, competitive market forces are allowed to function properly and true business value is established. I am often asked by a business owner what he should do when he is approached by an unsolicited offer. As a general rule, these buyers are only interested if they can get a bargain and limit the process to themselves as the only buyer.

First question I would ask the potential seller is, do you know the value of your business? If he says yes, my next question would be, how do you know? Have you had a recent valuation? Are you familiar with other comparable transactions? Are there rule of thumb valuation multiples for your business? Are you aware of any strategic value components your company may possess? Are you familiar with a discounted cash flow and terminal value approach to valuation?

If he feels comfortable with the value of his business, would this value be adequate for his financial future? What if a buyer was willing to meet his value criteria, but the seller were asked to take some as an earn out or some as a seller note? What offer would induce this owner to change his exit plans, assuming he was not already for sale?

In most cases, the buyer is very aware of the market and the owner is not nearly as well informed. The buyer most likely has made similar overtures to three to six other companies and is attempting to bring one bargain to closing. Because he has multiple opportunities, he has the leverage.

When talking to business owners who have gone through this unfortunate dance with a single buyer, several patterns repeat themselves. The first is that the seller is unable to pin the buyer down on the price and terms even after several months of buyer tire kicking. They are vague and evasive. They reschedule and delay meetings. They drag the process out. They introduce a partner deep into the process who starts hacking away at the terms and the deal shrinks. They discover minor issues in due diligence and act like there should be deal term and price adjustments. The seller gets deal fatigue.

The single buyer is emotionally detached from this process and thinks it is just part of his deal making skill. He is doing the same thing with multiple business owners simultaneously who have a much different emotional connection to the product of their life's work. The buyer is behaving badly and the owner really has no leverage to make the buyer behave. Most of the time the owner will simply blow up the deal after wasting months of time and a great deal of emotional strain. Sometimes he just caves in and sells out at the newly adjusted lower price. What a terrible outcome.

How should the business owner handle this? First answer is my company is not for sale. That usually scares the bottom feeders off because you are establishing a point of strength that you do not need to sell. Of course the buyer will say that everything is for sale. The next step would be to get mutual non disclosures executed and if you are sharing financials, you have the right to request his financials to make sure he has the financial ability to afford you. If it is a public company, you can check the public records for financials.

You really do not want to let the potential buyer do much more looking until he has submitted a qualified letter of intent. That basically says that if we do our due diligence and find out that everything you have told us checks out and we do not find any material surprises, we are willing to pay this much and on these terms for your company. Why would you let another company tear yours apart without knowing that their offer is acceptable to you once they do?

These are good steps, but I still have not solved your problem, leverage. You only have one buyer and you really have no pricing or negotiating leverage. For that you need multiple buyers. A business owner who has to run his business, which is already more than a full time job, normally can only process one buyer at a time. Therefore no leverage, no pricing power, no competition, no good result.

For that you need multiple buyers. To accomplish that you need a merger and acquisition advisor or business broker or investment banker, depending on the size and complexity of the potential transaction. When we are contacted by an owner that has one of these buyers in pursuit, we simply throw that buyer in to the process. When it becomes evident that this is going to become a competitive buying process, they head for easier territory pretty quickly. In our many years of doing this and in the twenty five year history of my prior firm, in only one case did the original unsolicited buyer end up being the winner. And that final price was 35% greater than his original offer.

The unsolicited offer is originally attractive to

the business owner because he believes that he will net much more from the transaction if he can avoid paying the investment banking fees. The practical reality is that being sort of, kind of for sale will depreciate your company's value. Either tell these buyers to go away completely or tell them you will have your investment banker contact them. This one buyer middle ground is not a good place for you or your company.

5.3 – Business Sellers Often Suffer from Single Buyer Syndrome

Remember when you were a child and your mother told you not to touch the hot stove? You couldn't really appreciate that message until you felt the pain shoot through your entire body by way of your finger tips. Oh, now I understand. Sometimes our prospective business sellers get the same kind of message as they pursue the sale of their business to a buyer who approached them with an unsolicited interest to buy.

We often get an inquiry from this business owner because this is usually the only time he will sell a company. He wants advice from us and his position is that he will hire our firm to represent him if this buyer falls through. Really the best advice we can give him is to engage our firm and let us throw this buyer into the mix of potential buyers that we will uncover. His response is almost always, I just want to see how this buyer plays out. We have watched this movie that I will call the Single Buyer Syndrome, a hundred times, so let me describe how it plays out.

- The potential buyer begins an exhaustive courting and informal due diligence process without any offer or Letter of Intent.

- The owner takes his eye off the ball, counting his millions prematurely and devotes less attention than usual in running his business.

- The buyer draws out the process by delaying and rescheduling meetings. He does not treat this process with the same focus and sense of urgency that the seller is now consumed with. Do you know why? The buyer is doing the same dance with 3 or 4 other prospective acquisitions.

- The seller has a difficult time getting the

buyer to put some terms and conditions in writing. If he does, it provides a good deal of wiggle room to adjust his offer as due diligence progresses.

• The process seems to stretch on and on as more meetings get delayed and rescheduled.

• Finally, the seller gets aggravated and begins to put some time limits and demands on the buyer.

• The buyer now gathers his team of accountants, attorneys, operations managers, and others to tear apart your company.

• This team finds all kinds of problems that they use to justify lowering the offer and increasing the reps and warranties and increasing the amount of hold back in an escrow account. They also bring up the requirement for owner financing for the first time.

• The buyer has carved a significant chunk

out of his offer while using all his experts to back him up. The seller is now 6 months into the process and the buyer knows that you have a great deal of skin in the game. He is counting on the seller to just cave and weakly counter because this process has just worn him down.

• If the seller relents, he likely has had his original offer reduced by 20% or more. The original offer, however, started below what the business was actually worth. If he sells under these circumstances, he likely will realize 30% or more below what a fair market competitive bid situation would produce.

• The other response from the seller is to be insulted and blow up the deal, leaving his company in a weaker state than when this whole process began. The seller focused much of his own energy on this process rather than running his business.

• The buyer moves on to his next acquisition candidate with the same M.O.

Unfortunately, the story does not end here. Many owners will go through this process more than once. It can stretch on for years because he can normally process only one buyer at a time. The only way to insure the right selling price is to throw these buyers into a formal M&A process. When you do, these buyers usually drop out of the running pretty quickly because they want to find a bargain. You worked too long and too hard to suffer from Single Buyer Syndrome and sell your company for a discount.

5.4 – The Unsolicited Offer to Buy Your Company -What Should You Do

If you are approached with an unsolicited offer to buy your business, be careful. Often times it is a bottom feeder looking to get a bargain and your company is one of dozens that are similarly contacted. If you become intoxicated with the thoughts of future riches, you could put your company in jeopardy. This article examines how you should manage this process.

When a company approaches you and broaches the subject of acquiring your company, it is very difficult to suppress those feelings of riches beyond your wildest dreams. Your thoughts start to move from the twelve hour work days, personnel issues, keeping your clients happy, and drift toward the tropical island with the grass hut, the perfect climate, the umbrella drinks, and the abundant leisure time. Snap out of it! Put that Champaign away and get back to reality.

We had been engaged by a client to sell her business recently and while we were in the planning meeting, the assistant walked in with a letter from a larger industry player expressing an interest in buying her company. She was feeling pretty special until we uncovered that this same letter was sent out to 50 other companies. Buyers are looking to buy at a discount if possible. The way they do that is similar to the approach that many of those get rich quick real estate programs recommend. Go out to 50 sellers and make a low-ball offer and one of them may bite. These buyers are way better informed about the value of a company than 90% of the business owners they approach.

The odds of a deal closing in this unsolicited approach are pretty slim. In the real estate example, the home owner is not hurt by one of these approaches, because they have a good idea of the value of their home. The price offer comes in immediately and they recognize it as a low ball and send the buyer packing. For the business owner, however, valuations are not that simple. This is the start of the death spiral. I don't want to sound overly dramatic, but this rarely has a happy ending. These supposed buyers will not give you a price offer. They drain your time, resources, your focus on running your business and, your company's performance. They want to buy your business as the only bidder and get a big discount. They will kick your tires, kick your tires, and kick your tires some more.

If they finally get to an offer after months of this resource drain, it is woefully short of expectations, to the surprise or chagrin of the owner. The owner became intoxicated with their vision of riches and took their eye off the ball of running their business.

How should you handle this situation so you do not have this outcome? We suggest that you do not let an outside force determine your selling timeframe. However, we recognize that everything is for sale at the right price. That is the right starting point. Get the buyer to sign a confidentiality agreement. Provide income statement, balance sheet and your yearly budget and forecast. Determine what is that number that you would accept as your purchase price and present that to the buyer. You may put it like this, " We really were not considering selling our company, but if you want us to consider going through the due diligence process, we will need an offer of $6.5 million. If you are not prepared to give us a LOI at that level, we are not going to entertain further discussions."

A second approach would be to ask for that number and if they were willing to agree, then you would agree to begin the due diligence process. If they were not, then you were going to engage your merger and acquisition advisor and they would be welcome to participate in the process with the other buyers that were brought into the process.

A major mistake business owners make in this situation is to focus their time and attention on selling the business as opposed to running the business. This occurs in large publicly traded companies with deep management teams as well as in private companies where management is largely in the hands of a single individual. Many large companies that are in the throes of being acquired are guilty of losing focus on the day-to-day operations. In case after case these businesses suffer a significant competitive downturn. If the acquisition does not materialize, their business has suffered significant erosion in value.

For a privately held business the impact is even more acute. There simply is not enough time for the owner to wear the many hats of operating his business while embarking on a full-time job of selling his business. Going through an extended process with a buyer who only wanted to buy at a bargain can damage the small company. If you are not for sale, you must control the process. Why would you go through the incredible resource drain before you knew if the offer would be acceptable? Get a qualified letter of intent on the front end or send this buyer packing.

5.5 – I Want to Sell my Company, - Just After This Next Big Sale

If you are waiting for that next big deal before you sell your company, you may want to re think your approach. An intelligent structure may be the way to help you capture the most value. You have made the decision to sell your company. Maybe it was because a major company in a related industry just acquired a direct competitor. It could be that one of the industry giants recently acquired one of your small but worthy competitors and has removed the risk component of a buyer's decision. Maybe your fire to compete at your top level is not burning as brightly as it once did.

These are all good reasons to set your business sale process in motion. A critical element here is time. Given this scenario, the more rapidly you can get your acquisition opportunity in front of the viable buyers, the better your chance for more favorable sale terms and conditions.

All systems go, right? But wait. We have a major proposal out to that Blue Chip account and when we get that deal our sale price will sky rocket. So we are just going to wait for that deal to close and then put our company up for sale.

Let me give you a gem here. We will call it the Moving Sales Pipeline Theorem. It states the sales pipeline always moves to the right. This is based on over 20 years in sales and sales management experience and many years of selling companies with sales pipelines. The sales either take much longer than projected or do not materialize at all.

Given this, the time critical nature of your pending business sale, and your desire to ring the bell from your Blue Chip account deal, what do you do?

You engage a great M&A firm that specializes in selling similar companies (I know of one if you are interested) to sell your business. Let them focus on selling your business and you focus on running your business and closing that big sale. Get several buyers interested and negotiate for your best deal. There will be a lot of give and take here. At the right moment, as a counter to one of the buyer's points, you ask for a 6-month window post acquisition to close that deal. You then ask, for example, for an earn out incentive of 30% of the contracted first year revenues of the Blue Chip account deal as "additional transaction value" payable 30 days after the one year purchase anniversary date.

There are lots of moving parts here so let me elaborate. The first element is you do not delay your business sale process. We already established that it was time critical. Secondly, I very carefully chose the language "additional transaction value". We want to make sure that this payment is not confused with ordinary income at double the long term capital gains tax rate. Third, you have a way better chance of closing the big Blue Chip account as a division of G. E., for example, than as XYZ Manufacturing, Inc. Finally, what a great way to kick off a relationship than a big collaborative sales win that makes the buyer look really smart. Your earn out check will be the most enjoyable payment they can make.

5.6 – How Not to Sell Your Business

Ask any business owner who has sold a business or attempted to sell a business, "What would you do differently?" If he or she attempted to sell it without help, chances are pretty good that the transaction did not succeed. If the transaction were actually completed, chances are that they did not get a good price, but had no idea that this occurred.

We were recently engaged to sell a medical products company. In our process we will identify 50 to 150 companies that would be likely buyers based on similar products, services or markets served. When those targets are approved by our seller client, we get on the phone and contact the buying prospect to see if we can generate some interest and get confidentiality agreements executed.

We were able to identify several interested buyers and were at the stage where they were submitting their qualified Letters of Intent. The LOI basically says that if we complete our due diligence and we find that everything is as you earlier presented it, we will pay you $XXX under these terms and conditions.

We got one offer from a perfect fit buyer and we determined that it was well short of our seller's expectations and well below what our view of the price for similar companies in this market niche. We called this buyer to discuss his offer.

When we told him our client's range of expectations, he said that it was way too expensive. We asked him what basis he had for that conclusion, he replied that he was looking to pay 5 X Cash Flow for a business. We told him that recent transactions indicated that similar companies were selling for 2.5 times revenues and not a price based on a cash flow model.

Let's take this a little further with some ball park calculations based on our transaction. For example, if our client had $5 million in revenue and a 20% cash flow margin, his cash flow is $1 million and according to this buyer, his company should sell for 5 X $1 million or $5 million. The market view, however, is that this company is worth $5 million X 2.5 or $12.5 million. When we dug a little deeper into our buyer's offer we found out that he currently was in the process of buying another similar company.

When we inquired for more detail we found

that this other company was a long time competitor, the owner was getting ready to retire and approached this buyer to see if he would be interested in acquiring them. We asked the buyer if the seller was represented by an investment banker, business broker or merger and acquisition advisor. He said that the seller was not. I asked him if there were any other buyers involved in the process. He said that as far as he knew, he was the only buyer. I asked him how the selling price was determined. The buyer said that he set the price based on, you guessed it, 5 X cash flow.

Let's see what this seller's approach is going to cost him. If we assume that he was very similar in size and cash flow to our client. A competitive market price in a formal merger and acquisition process would be $12.5 million. Our buyer will pay him only $5 million and the seller will close thinking he got a fair deal without any market validation. This is a $7.5 million mistake that could have very easily been avoided by hiring a business sales professional that would have invited in multiple buyers and multiple competitive bids.

Well, at least the seller avoided all investment banker fees. This is a sad end to a 25 year history of business excellence. Unfortunately it happens all the time.

5.7 – Management Buyout

Many owners think that selling their privately held company to their management team is a great way to reward loyal employees for years of service. We will present why that seldom works and put forth another approach that is a better alternative for owners, employees, and the buyers.

Many business owners want to thank their loyal employees that have helped them build their businesses when they exit. It is a noble desire that often leads to the exploration of a management buyout. Who better to buy the business than the management team that is familiar with the procedures, the customers, the suppliers, the industry and the intellectual property?

From a practical standpoint, however, unless the potential management buyout team already owns a meaningful percentage of the company, it is unlikely they have the financial resources to complete the acquisition. These managers may be great employees, but they generally do not have the risk tolerance to put their personal assets at stake in order to finance the acquisition.

They may originally think that they will be able to secure financing to make the acquisition. When they begin to peel back the layers they find that their enthusiasm begins to crack. Banks are not going to finance an acquisition based on a competitive market price for the business. They will make loans based on a percentage of the asset value of the equipment, receivables and inventory that exceed the company's debt level. This will likely result in the buyout group getting financing at 40-50% of the true value of the company.

Where does the rest come from? When the management buyout team explores the effective rate of mezzanine financing – 12% interest rate with warrants that drive the cost to 25%, they usually eliminate that option. The next option is the personal assets of the team. When the banks start asking for personal guarantees, individuals drop out pretty quickly.

This process sometimes evolves to the owner being asked to settle for a purchase price closer to the secured financing level available rather than the market value of the company. On a company with a $10 million fair market value, this could result in a discount of $5 million or more. I am sure the business owner is grateful to his loyal employees, but this is just not practical.

The problem occurs after this process unfolds and the once very excited management team realizes that their dream of ownership has been knocked off the track. If some of the key players blame the owner, they can turn from loyal to disgruntled and may even leave the company. This can result in erosion in company value in the eyes of the eventual buyer. The original noble plan has blown up in the owner's face.

Another approach would be for the owner to engage an investment banker to seek competitive bids from both strategic buyers and private equity groups. This process will establish the true market value that will be far superior to the financing value of the assets minus liabilities. The owner could grant key employees a cash award based on years of service, salary, or other criteria of his choice.

If the buyer is a Private Equity Group, the owner has another option that may be even more attractive to key employees and the Owner. PEGs encourage sellers to invest some of their equity back into the business. They get to invest leveraged equity along with the PEG.

So let's say that the selling price of the business was $10 million. The PEG would borrow $7 million and need $3 million in equity. If the seller invests $1 million of his proceeds back into the business, he would own 33% of the new entity. If the owner was planning on distributing $500,000 to employees, he could reinvest that $500,000 along with his $500,000 back into the business and he would then own 16 ½% and the employees would own 16 ½% of the new entity.

This works out for everybody because the employees will be highly motivated to stay and to 0perform at a high level for their eventual exit and cash out. The PEG gets to keep a performing management team in place that is highly motivated. The owner gets the maximum selling price for his business because of the soft auction business selling process. Finally, the owner gets to reward his loyal employees with a powerful investment in their future.

The second payoff for the owner and the powerful payoff for the employees comes five years later when the PEG sells the company now valued at $50 million to a strategic industry buyer. This second bite of the apple values the owner's retained 16 ½% stake at $8,250,000. The loyal employees cash out at that same level from an original $500,000 bonus. Now that's a bonus!

5.8 – The Number One Cause of M&A Deal Failures

I believe one of the biggest reasons for M&A deals blowing up is a poorly worded Letter of Intent. The standard process is to solicit offers from buyers in the form of Letters of Intent (LOI). The terms and conditions are negotiated until one winner emerges and the seller and buyer dual sign the LOI which is non-binding. This basically gives either party an out should something be discovered in the due diligence process that is not to their liking or is not as presented in the initial materials.

When I say poorly worded, what I really should have said is that it is worded much to the advantage of the buyer and gives them a lot of wiggle room in how the letter is interpreted and translated into the definitive purchase agreement. The best comparison I can make is a lease agreement for an apartment. It is so one-sided in favor of the landlord and protects him from every conceivable problem with the renter.

Business buyers are usually very experienced and the sellers are generally first time sellers. The buyers have probably learned some important and costly lessons from past deals and vow never to let that happen again. This is often reflected in their LOI. They also count on several dynamics from the process that are in their favor. Their deal team is experienced and is at the ready to claim that "this is a standard deal practice" or "this is the calculation according to GAAP accounting rules". They count on the seller suffering from deal fatigue after the numerous conference calls, corporate visits, and the arduous production of due diligence information.

When the LOI is then translated into the Definitive Purchase Agreement by the buyer's team, any term that is open for interpretation will be interpreted in favor of the buyer and conversely to the detriment of the seller. The seller can try to fight each point, and usually there are several attacks on the original value detailed in the dual signed LOI that took the seller off the market for 45-60 days. The buyer and his team of experts will fight each deal term from the dispassionate standpoint on one evaluating several deals simultaneously. The seller, on the other hand, is fully emotionally committed to the result of his life's work. He is at a decided negotiating disadvantage.

The unfortunate result of this process is that the seller usually caves on most items and sacrifices a significant portion of the value that he thought he would realize from the sale. More often than not, however, the seller interprets this activity by the buyer as acting in bad faith and simply blows up the deal, only to return to the market as damaged goods. The implied message when we reconnect with previous interested buyers after going into due diligence is that the buyers found some dirty laundry in the process. These previously interested buyers may jump back in, but they generally jump back in at a transaction value lower than what they were originally willing to pay.

How do we stop this unfortunate buyer advantage and subsequent bad behavior? The first and most important thing we can do is to convey the message that there are several interested and qualified buyers that are very close in the process. If we are doing our job properly, we will be conveying an accurate version of the reality of the deal. The message is that we have many good options and if you try to behave badly, we will simply cut you off and reach out to our next best choices. The second thing we can do is to negotiate the wording in the Letter of Intent to be very precise and not allow room for interpretation that can attack the value and terms we originally intended. We will show a couple examples of LOI deal points as written by the buyer (with lots of room for interpretation) and we will counter those with examples of precise language that protects the seller.

Buyer's Earnout Language:

The amount will be paid using the following formula:

-75% of the value will be paid at closing

-The remaining 25% will be held as retention by the BUYERs to be paid in 2 equal installments at the 12 month and 24 month anniversaries, based on the following formula and with the goal of retaining at least 95% of the TTM revenue. In case at the 12 and 24 month anniversaries the TTM revenue falls below 95%, the retention amount will be adjusted based on the percentage retained. For example, if 90% of the TTM revenue is retained at 12 months, the retention value will be adjusted to 90% of the original value. In case the revenue retention falls at or below 80%, the retention value will be adjusted to $0.

Earnout Language Seller Counter Proposal

The amount will be paid using the following formula:

-75% of the value will be paid at closing

-The remaining 25% will be held as Earnout by the BUYERs to be paid in 4 equal installments at the 6, 12, 18 and 24 months anniversaries, based on the following formula:

We will set a 5% per year revenue growth target for two years as a way for Sellers to receive 100% of their Earnout (categorized as "additional transaction value" for contract and tax purposes).

So, for example, the trailing 12 months revenues for the period above for purposes of this example are $2,355,000. For a 5% growth rate in year one, the resulting target is $2,415,000 for year 1 and $2,535,750 in year 2. The combined revenue target for the two years post acquisition is $4,950,750.

Based on a purchase price of $2,355,430, the

25% earnout would be valued at par at $588,857. We can simply back into an earnout payout rate by dividing the par value target of $588,857 by the total targeted revenues of $4.95 MM.

The result is a payout rate of 11.89% of the first two years' revenue. If SELLER falls short of the target they fall short in the payout, if they exceed the amount, they earn a payout premium. Below are two examples of performance:

Example 1 is the combined 2 years' revenues total $4.50 MM - the resulting 2 year payout would be $535,244.

Example 2 is the combined 2 years' revenues total $5.50 MM - the resulting 2 year payout would be $654,187.

Comparison and Comments: The buyer's language contained a severe penalty if revenues dropped below 80% of prior levels, the earnout payment goes to $0. Also they have only a penalty for falling short and no corresponding reward for exceeding expectations. The seller's counter proposal is very specific, formula driven and uses examples. It will be very hard to misinterpret this language. The seller's language accounts for the punishment of a shortfall with the upside reward of exceeding growth projections. The principle of both proposals is the same - to protect and grow revenue, but the results for the seller are far superior with the counter proposal language.

Buyer's Working Capital Example:

This proposal assumes a cash free, debt free balance sheet and a normalized level of working capital at closing.

Seller's Working Capital Counter Proposal:

At or around closing the respective accounting teams will do an analysis of accounts payable and accounts receivable. The seller will retain all receivables in excess of payables plus all cash and cash equivalents. The balance sheet will be assumed by the buyer with a $0 net working capital balance.

Comparison and Comments: The buyer's language is vague and not specific and is a problem waiting to happen. So for example, if the buyer's experts decide that a "normalized level of working capital at closing is a surplus of $400,000, the value of the transaction to the seller dropped by $400,000 compared to the seller's counter proposal language. The objective in seller negotiations is to truly understand the value of the various offers before countersigning the LOI. For example, an offer for cash at closing of $4,000,000 with the seller retaining all excess net working capital when the normal level is $800,000 is superior to an offer for $4.4 million with working capital levels retained at normal levels.

These are two very important deal terms and they can move the effective transaction value by large amounts if they are allowed to be loosely worded in the letter of intent and then interpreted to the buyer's advantage in translation to the definitive purchase agreement. Why not just cut off that option with very precise and specific language in the LOI with formulas and examples prior to execution by the seller. The chances of the deal going through to closing will rise dramatically with this relatively easy to execute negotiation element.

5.9 – Don't Allow the Process to Derail the Deal

Most business owners sell only one business in

their lifetime. It is complex, emotional and pressure packed. Given this backdrop, the odds of a great outcome are, well, not that great.

One of our most important functions is to prepare our client for the bumpy road ahead. The worst outcome is to go through the exhaustive process of marketing the business, corporate visits, and due diligence, only to have the deal crater in month eight because of some ruffled feathers or perceived bad faith dealings.

First we try to make the seller understand that as the process unfolds and as the buyer tries to memorialize the parties' understanding in documents, new elements are added. For example, taking a discussion between buyer and seller on value may be followed with a "non-binding" letter of intent where for the first time, the structure is described. The seller may react very negatively if he was thinking of a $7 million wire transfer at closing and the written document combines $4 million cash at close with a $1 million seller note and an earn out that caps out at $2 million. If we had not earlier forced the issue or warned our seller that this was a possibility, then maybe we deserved to have an unhappy client. Our goal is to turn this from a "he changed the transaction" deal breaker to a couple of deal points that we negotiate.

Another sticky point if the seller is not prepared is the concept of the net working capital adjustment. This is a customary deal approach from experienced buyers that is fair. Trying to explain it to the seller for the first time during the heat of battle can be problematic. In advance we tell our seller that the buyer is going to want a measuring point based on the latest financials he receives in order to make his offer. If, at that point, the current assets are $350 K and the current liabilities are $300 K then the company has net working capital of $50 K. If that level changes then at the post closing true-up, an adjustment will be made to account for the change.

If a seller is not prepared for the pages of reps and warranties that are a standard part of most Definitive Purchase Agreements, the initial reaction is often, "no way." It is, however, a deal breaker for buyers, especially if they are public companies. With the new corporate governance scrutiny, these companies are very meticulous about protecting themselves.

The next potential stumbling block is when the buyer's corporate attorney gets involved to make sure that the mother ship is protected. It happened at the 11th hour and the way it was handled by the buyer almost blew up the deal. We had settled on the terms and conditions of the transaction and had worked out a 12-month consulting contract with the founder of the selling company. The senior management of the buyer detailed the duties and responsibilities in a "consulting agreement." When their corporate attorney received this document, he said that it is not a consulting agreement, but an employment agreement. Our client did not want to go from being a CEO to now being a VP. It was a drop in prestige for her and did not fit the image she had created for herself post acquisition. We had to talk her off the ledge and had to convince her that this should not be a deal breaker. We had to remind her that this buyer was the best fit for her company and she had the best opportunity of maximizing her earn out portion of the transaction with this buyer.

We convinced her to sleep on it. We also enlisted the support of her CFO, husband and dear friend (all the same person). We were able to enlist his calm logical thought process and convince his wife that this was a relatively small impact, all things considered. She agreed.

Wait, you thought this was settled. Not so fast. Enter the Business Development/ Merger and Acquisition person from the buyer (BD). He attempts to push the deal through without adding employee benefits to the employment agreement because those benefits were not figured into his original financial analysis. He got very protective of his turf and made this counter proposal without consulting his President and EVP. Our client went ballistic. We literally had to walk her out of the conference room and cancelled the closing meeting until the next day.

We had already done two end runs around BD and we were worried that if we did a third we may cause doubt about the post acquisition behavior of our client in the eyes of the buyer president, or worse, cause BD to blow the deal up because we bruised his ego.

Well, we got lucky. The next day, before our meeting was due to begin, we ran into an individual doing a walk through at our client's offices. We introduced ourselves and asked her who she was. She replied that she was the head of HR for the buying company. We asked her if they typically had two classes of employees, one with benefits and one without. She looked at us incredulously and asked us what we were talking about. We explained and she said she would have it cleared up by the end of the day. She also gave our client her card and scheduled a call with her so she could implement the full package of employee benefits. Fast forward – BD has been moved out of the M&A position.

We had spent a tremendous amount of our client's time, the buying executives' time and our time and everyone involved knew that this was a good and fair transaction. With all of the pressure, emotion, and egos involved, sometimes even good deals do not get completed. You need experienced advisors that operate in the role of "shepherd of the deal" to guide the transaction through closing.

CHAPTER 6

Important Elements of the Business Sale Process

6.1 – Experience Trumps Smarts in the Sale of Your Company

People who start software and information technology companies are generally very smart people. When it comes to representing yourself in the sale of your business, the key issue is not smarts, but experience. Our purpose here is to explore the intelligence versus experience issue and give examples where experience trumps intelligence.

The greater the complexity of the task, the more

the advantage goes to the one who has prior experience with that task. Ask anyone who has sold their business and they will tell you it is a surprisingly complex undertaking.

Some very well-known examples were the experiences of the great author, George Plimpton as he stepped into the boxing ring against Joe Louis, put on the goalie pads for the Boston Bruins or barked out signals as the quarterback for the Detroit Lions in a pre-season football game.

These experiences resulted in some great reading. The competitive outcome for the inexperienced combatant, however, was not a happy ending. Curious George was totally outmatched. Admittedly, I had earlier written self-serving articles and Blog posts on the benefits of business seller representation by a Merger and Acquisition Advisor or Business Broker. There are hundreds of similar articles out there from our competitors. The message is pretty much the same:

1. They know the market and the valuations.

2. They have an active database of identified buyers.

3. By representing yourself, you alert the market, your customers, your competitors, and your employees that you are for sale.

4. Running a business is a full-time job. Selling a business is also a full-time job.

5. A business owner normally conducts a serial process (one buyer at a time) which dramatically reduces his market feedback and negotiating position.

6. It is complex, you may only sell one business in your lifetime and the buyers are much more experienced than the sellers.

I really want to dissect point number 6 because I don't believe most business owners fully embrace either the complexity or the consequences of the disparity in experience. First of all, as a generalization, successful business owners are really smart people and have solved myriad complex problems over the years to make their businesses prosper. To many of them, selling their business is just another of those complex problems that they have routinely solved to their advantage. Well, I am a pretty smart guy (my kids might differ), but if my doctor presented me with my lab test results from my physical and asked me to prescribe my treatment, I would refer him to a mental health professional. The point here is not my intelligence, but my level of experience.

Joe Louis spent 10,000 hours perfecting his craft under extreme conditions of competition and pressure. George Plimpton worked in a gym for a couple of weeks with a boxing trainer. If you asked Joe Louis to write a Pulitzer Prize winning novel, you might have to duck a right cross. Both Joe Louis and George Plimpton were geniuses at their craft. They were inexperienced in other areas and were at a distinct disadvantage when trying to compete in another field against the experts in that field.

As I retrieve my third golf ball from the water hazard, I rationalize to myself, "Well at least Tiger Woods can't run an HP 12C present value calculator like I can. Knowing Tiger Woods, he actually probably can.

Let me try another example of the value of experience to illustrate my point. Have you ever tried mounting a new door? The first time I did it, it took me several hours - getting the special hole drill for the knob and internal mechanism, measuring for hinges, chiseling the slots for the hinges, propping the door and securing it for mounting, etc. Each one of these steps was something new to me and I wasn't very good at any of them. By my third door mounting, I was starting to become pretty competent. For a business owner, your business sale is your first door. By the way, that is one very important door.

Now let's look at the buyers. The first category is the Private Equity Investor. They buy businesses for a living. Ask an average PEG (Private Equity Group) how many deals they look at for every one they actually acquire. They will tell you it is well over 200 different companies. Most of these 200 are dismissed at the start of the process with the teaser or blind profile. They can judge whether the target meets their broad criteria of revenue, EBITDA, profit margins, industry segment, and others.

Many businesses pass their initial screen and they enter the excruciating process of conference calls, detailed data requests on customers, vendors, gross profit by product/customer/vendor, sales by product/customer, top ten customers, top 10 suppliers, percentage of business in the top ten, and on-

and on. Many more companies are eliminated in this process. We then proceed to the indication of interest letter (broad statement of the economics of their proposed deal) followed by corporate visits. Once through that process, the surviving targets get additional data requests and follow-up questions. This is not always a one-way elimination. Sometimes the PEG IOI letter is not high enough to make the seller's cut and they will be eliminated from the process.

The home stretch is submitting a Letter of Intent with a much tighter presentation of the final deal value and structure. This is a competitive process and the seller winnows the suitors down to 1 finalist through back and forth negotiations. Once the highest and best LOI is countersigned by the seller, there is an exclusive period for due diligence. Often the deal blows up in due diligence when a material issue is uncovered and the buyer attempts to alter their original offer in response to this new data. Often times the seller will simply blow up the deal. So the process starts all over.

The point here is that these Private Equity Groups have vast experience, not only in closing deals, but vast experience with every stage of the deal process. So for every deal completed they originally look at 200 teasers that result in the execution of 50 confidentiality agreements and the review of 50 memoranda. 20 of those deals warrant a conference call with the owners and follow up questions. 8 companies survive that process and result in 8 indications of interest letters and 5 corporate visits. 3 companies survive to due diligence and 1 makes it to the finish line. This is a continual moving pipeline of deep deal experience.

As a business owner, by the time you connect with a PEG, they have pretty much seen every twist and turn a deal can take. Their approach resembles an apartment owner's rental agreement - tremendously one-sided in their favor. For a PEG, a deal that blows up in the eleventh hour becomes an expensive lesson learned and war story. For a business owner, it can dramatically negatively impact their future business performance.

Wait, you say. I am a software company with the next big thing. My buyer is not a private equity group, but one of the strategic buyers - IBM, Google, Facebook, Adobe, and Microsoft (pick your giant). Let me give you a humbling dose of reality. We have represented some world class technology companies and just getting one of these blue chippers to take a look at them is a monumental task. The primary objective of the M&A department of the giants is to protect the mother ship. They want to prevent entrepreneurs from getting into any potential legal claim on the Blue Chip's intellectual property.

Therefore they institute a screening process designed to surround the company with a corporate moat around the castle. That moat has different names at each company. At one it is called the "Opportunity Management System". At another it is the "Partnership Management Department".

Here is how it works. The individuals in this department are very hard to find and very seldom answer their phone. You are directed to a Website and are required to fill out an exhaustive 16 page submission form. You are then issued a submission number. You then go into the black hole and may be reviewed by a junior level screener that does not have the breadth of experience to judge a Twitter versus a Pets.com.

It gets worse. Every day 100 more "Opportunities" get submitted and piled on top of your number. The only way to get attention is from the Division Manager who owns the functional area where your product fits. Convince him to go rescue your number and to get your form to a senior opportunity manager to process and vet the idea.

Just like with the PEGs, this is a relentless process of deal flow for these company buyers. Sellers in this environment are on their heels right from the start and struggle to garner any negotiating leverage. If your technology is strong enough to be rescued for a more comprehensive look, the guys on the other side of the table are the heavyweight champions of M&A deals. They have seen it all.

Not to minimize the first 5 benefits identified earlier in this article, but balancing the experience of the buyer's team with the experience of the seller's team is critical to enhance, protect and preserve the value of your transaction.

In its purest form, a letter of intent is a document designed to define the economic parameters of a transaction that, pending completion of due diligence, will be memorialized in a definitive purchase agreement and a deal closing. In its practical use, a letter of intent is like an apartment renter's agreement with every subtle advantage benefitting the author of the document. An inexperienced seller will agree to a seemingly innocuous clause about working capital adjusted at closing according to GAAP accounting rules. If you are the seller of a software company with annual software licenses or prepaid maintenance contracts, that could be a $ million mistake. It is a rare attorney that would ever catch that. Well, not actually. They are all representing the experienced buyers.

6.2 – Make Sure You Find the Right Buyers

We are in the middle of a merger and acquisition engagement representing a Human Resources Consulting Company. We had contacted several industry players and had gotten some good initial interest. Several buyers dropped out because their entire management team was comprised of family members. We asked our client to take their company off the market and to bring in at least one non family executive that had the authority and the ability to run the company. They successfully implemented this change and asked us to take them back out to market.

Because their business is counter cyclical and actually grew during the economic downturn they posted some pretty impressive growth and profit numbers. It was difficult to determine how much of the improvement was due to the addition of the new senior manager.

As we re-launched our marketing efforts, we identified several interested buyers. One buyer was particularly interested and after signing the confidentiality agreement and reviewing the memorandum, contacted us almost daily with additional detailed information requests. Before long he started to grill us about selling price expectations. As we usually do, we deflected his requests and asked him to put together his letter of intent based on the value of the business to his company.

He started giving us a lecture about valuing services companies whose assets (meaning people) walked out the door every evening. He pointed out that their revenues were based on new sales each year and not "contractually recurring revenue". We had our client put together for us a chart that showed the "historically recurring revenue" generated from their top 20 clients over the past five years. This was our way to demonstrate some consistency and predictability of revenues.

As we conversed further, my radar started buzzing loudly. This guy was getting ready to provide a low ball offer and was trying to sell me on all the reasons why I should go back to our client and pitch his offer. I politely listened to his well practiced approach for a little while longer. Then he came up with the statement that I just could not let go. He said that last year's revenues were an unusual upward spike and "I am just going to use 2015's revenues as my basis for my offer. Well, I just could not let that one go. I asked him how he would have made an offer if last year was unusually bad, but the prior five years were strong. He would not respond, but of course, the answer was that he would have made his offer based on the new trend.

There are thousands of business buyers out there that are just like this guy. There is a famous residential real estate investor that has written a book and gives classes to help individuals become real estate moguls. I could sum up his book and his class in one sentence. Find 100 people with their homes for sale. Approach them aggressively and make a low ball offer and one of them will take it.

When I reviewed where our buyer had originated, I traced it back to a posting we had made on our business broker's association Web Site. As I think about it, these Business-for-Sale Web Sites actually give these buyers a powerful tool to actively and aggressively contact their 100 potential sellers. As I thought about this, sure enough, I have seen this behavior repeated multiple times and the source was always a Business-for-Sale Web Site.

So we are always preaching to our prospective clients to get multiple buyers involved in the process. If they post their business on one of the Business-for-Sale Web Sites, they may get multiple buyers interested, but they are those buyers that are contacting 100 sellers very efficiently through the power of the Internet in order to make their low ball offers.

But I digress. Let's get back to our client. The good news is that we had 6 other industry buyers that we had contacted and they were looking for acquisitions that were based on acquiring new customers or adding another product offering, or leveraging their sales force or install base. In other words, their buyer motivation was not to buy a company with a low-ball offer.

The only way we can encourage buyers to make fair offers is to conduct an outbound marketing campaign to industry buyers that have strategic reasons for making acquisitions. If we can get several involved, then the buyer that comes in and says that he is going to base his offer on 2008 performance, is easily eliminated from consideration. If a business seller is only going to attract these inbound, bargain seeker buyers from Web Sites, he/she will only be getting low ball offers and wasting a lot of time.

6.3 – A Major Concern for Technology Business Sellers –What Happens to My Employees

For family business owners, the employees, if they are not actually family, they are like family. Many have been there through the bad times and the good. They may have not gotten an expected raise because of tough times. They have been to each other's children's weddings. The boss has helped the employee family with an unexpected healthcare expense. The bonds are very strong. An admirable trait that we see from almost every business owner we represent is the deep concern for what happens to my employees when the new owner has our company.

The Hollywood portrayal of Mergers and Acquisitions on Wall Street is that the money guys come in and slash the staff, do their financial gymnastics, show impressive short term profits, and then flip the company to a new buyer and pocket millions on the backs of the loyal displaced employees. Does this really happen? Unfortunately is does happen, but the circumstances are generally the result of industries becoming bloated with legacy costs and wages and benefits at a level not competitive with the world economy. We have seen it with the steel industry, airlines, and now the auto industry.

However, for the family business, the backdrop is much different. The organizations are generally very lean. The employees are not constrained in their job description by union rules. They do what is necessary to get the job done. They often can perform multiple jobs and get plugged in where needed. Every employee is vital to the company's performance.

Business buyers are generally pretty smart folks. If they aren't, pretty soon they will find themselves in trouble from poor acquisition choices. They recognize the value that the employees bring to the table. These employees are keepers of the customer relationships, they are the well of knowledge about the company's products and competitive advantage, they know all the gotcha's to avoid. They are the new buyer's path to business continuity post acquisition and they are valued.

Business buyers look to mitigate risk by keeping these employees in place and will attempt to access the likelihood of key employees staying on post acquisition. We have heard from business buyers that if they feel like key employee A and key employee B leave, then we are not interested in the acquisition. As business sellers it is important to recognize this and to take necessary steps in advance of your sale to help the key employees stay.

At a point where the sale is ready to close, it is important to make sure employees have some reassurances that the ownership change will improve their situation. Often times the benefit package from the large company buyer is superior to the current package. Buyers will often incorporate a salary increase after the acquisition. Owners may elect to share some of their gains with key loyal employees through a stay on bonus or some lump sum payment recognizing the years of loyal service.

The finance and administrative area is the one exception to this rule. These functions are often a total duplication of those functions in the buying company and these employees are most vulnerable to a cut. These employees have contributed greatly to the company and have been loyal. The seller, unfortunately, can not dictate to the buyer that these employees have to be retained, so he must make accommodations on his own. He should attempt to get an understanding from the buyer, their plans for these employees and arrive at a joint proactive communication plan with the buyer. If the news is bad for the employee, the seller, at the very least should give the employee as much advanced notice as possible. The seller will often implement some severance package, if one was not already in place to give the displaced employee a chance to seek a new opportunity without financial hardship.

Most of the employees will be vital to the post acquisition success of the new company. If they interface with customers and/or suppliers they will be needed. If they are in possession of key knowledge about the company, products, industry, technology, etc., they will be valued and will have a solid job post sale.

6.4 – Understanding the Letter of Intent (LOI) in the Sale of a Business

The letter of intent is an essential step in facilitating the sale of a business. The purpose is to establish the economic framework for buyer and business seller to move to the due diligence phase. It basically says that with all the available information I have thus far seen and if that all stands the scrutiny of due diligence, I am willing to buy your business for X dollars under Y payment terms. It is however, non- binding pending the execution of mutually acceptable purchase agreements.

If I am a seller, I am going to insist that I have this letter establishing the economics of the deal before I agree to allow my company to be turned inside out with buyer staff and advisors. If, as the seller, I want $5 million and the LOI specifies $4.5 million, I am going to attempt to negotiate up before I counter sign this letter. If I am still short on price and terms, I continue to sell the company to other interested buyers.

If I am the buyer, I want the seller to commit to my economic parameters before I spend thousands going through due diligence. The other important element of the LOI from the buyer's perspective is exclusivity. The buyer will lock up this company for a period of from 30 days to 90 days to complete their due diligence and execute mutually agreeable definitive purchase agreements. That means that in return for the time, effort and expense of due diligence, the seller and his business broker or merger and acquisition advisor are not allowed to actively market the business to other interested parties.

If you are the seller and you get your LOI, don't celebrate yet. Make sure the financials that the buyer is analyzing to come up with his offer are professionally done using GAAP. Normally a measuring point is established in the LOI with those financials for net working capital. There will be an adjustment made to the transaction value (post closing adjustments) depending on the new net working capital balance post close.

If the buyer is looking at sales forecasts prior to submitting his LOI, make sure they are conservative and accurate. If you have some major sales losses or the pipeline moves to the right (they always do) some buyers may attempt to call that a material adverse change and look for an adjustment in purchase price.

Finally, the LOI is normally a three to seven page document without a lot of legal boilerplate. The purchase agreements that follow will take care of that. So expect 30 pages or more. Focus your efforts on the economic parameters and conserve your legal budget. You will need your attorney most for his help with the purchase agreements.

6.5 – Negotiations Can Be Too Personal

Making the decision to sell your business is hard enough, but having a buyer tell the owner it is not worth as much as he thought can really be a blow. The emotional attachment that most owners have to their business is very deep. They remember the long hours, the financial hardships, the wearing of all the hats responsibility, the worry and the pride of success. They believe that they ran their business the right way and that the new owners should stick with their system. With this backdrop, the actual selling and negotiating process can be a bucket of ice water over the head awakening - not at all pleasant.

Buyers and Sellers are at cross-purposes when it comes to the terms and conditions of a sale. What is positive for the buyer is negative for the seller and vice versa. When was the last time you bought a car and simply paid list price? For the car dealership, this back and forth haggling is simply part of the process. For a business owner, this process can feel like a personal attack. The owner's response to this perceived attack can often create a barrier to a successful transaction.

If you have ever followed the contract negotiation process between professional athletes and their team, you have a good example of how the process can often unfold with bad results. The team is trying to get the best deal, maintain fiscal responsibility, and manage to salary caps. The player is trying to get paid as much as he can and often uses the contract amount as his measure of worth in comparison to the other players in the league.

The team is trying to justify a lower salary and may bring up another player with superior stats and a lower salary as a negotiating point. They may point out one or two weaknesses in the player's game. The player holds out and misses games, hurting his team. He may respond to the negotiating tactics with attacks on the team's management in the newspapers. This process often creates irreparable damage and after a contentious year, the player is traded for far less than he was originally worth.

The emotions of a business seller are equally charged. If the buyer's offer is a fair deal and the owner wants it to occur, he must be able to detach his emotions from the normal negotiating process. Every point is not a personal attack. The buyer must understand that his intent in buying the company is to gain post acquisition performance improvement. If during the process, he values the last nickel he can scrape out of the deal at the expense of the good will of the selling company, he has defeated his purpose.

The use of intermediaries that are familiar with and comfortable with this process can keep the deal on track and preserve the necessary good relationship between the buyer and the seller. For the advisor, this is just part of the process and a point given by one side is exchanged for a point taken by the other. The transaction is completed, the two companies come together in a spirit of cooperation and growth and a year later both buyer and seller are happy with the result. After all, trading the acquired company to another team is not really an option.

6.6 – When You Sell Your Business Owner Perks Disappear

When representing business sellers it is important to recognize that this is usually their first and only experience in selling their business. No matter how smart they are, there is no replacement for experience in this complex process. Also, any mistakes made during this process are usually very expensive, time consuming or both. Finally, it is usually an emotional roller coaster for the owner - Am I doing the right thing? is this the right time? What is going to happen to my employees and my customers? Is this the right buyer? Are these the best price and terms I can get?

Because this process is so foreign and the emotions run so high, a seemingly simple action on the part of the buyer, if not anticipated and not prepared for, could disrupt or even blow up a mutually beneficial transaction. If our client gets surprised by a deal event and that event does some damage, I take that on as my responsibility. It takes only one deal to blow up to turn you into a serial client preparer.

To improve our odds of deal completion and success we make sure our clients are prepared for each stage of the deal, from the number one question - why are you selling, to the conference calls, corporate visits, frequently asked questions, letters of intent, buyer negotiations tactics, post closing adjustments, etc. The way we do this is every time we encounter something during a deal that our client should be prepared for or could cause an issue if not properly handled, we write a short article about it.

Then when we are coming up on a particular

deal element or deal stage, we send our client the article to read and then we discuss it with them. This is, very importantly, not reacting to the emotions during the heat of battle, but more like a run through practice prior to the big game. The team usually does better if they are prepared for the fake punt rather than experiencing it with the score tied with two minutes to go in the fourth quarter. So our dry run is done with no pressure, prior to the event, and most importantly, with emotions in check.

Just when I think that I have seen all the "gotchas" there are after fifteen years of grinding out deals, and that my article library was complete, we had a new issue come up which caused several hours of nervousness within the seller's team and the buyer's team.

We had all of the major deal terms worked out and detailed in a very comprehensive Letter of Intent and were requesting that the partner sellers countersign it to agree to go into quiet period and buyer due diligence.

One of the partners was completely on board but the other could not get his head around not retaining all of his owner perks - company lease on a luxury vehicle, fully paid cell phone, home internet service and a few others. For his future employment with the new company those would be handled at a much less generous and customary employee expense treatment.

I was a little taken aback by this and my first thought was, "is this guy going to blow up a deal for what amounts to less than one half of 1% of deal value? Then I remembered why we have written all of these articles. In the heat of battle, this guy was dealing with all of the emotions of turning his clients, employees, and even a good part of his identity for the past decade, over to a new caretaker. I really could not blame him for not displaying some good old fashioned emotionally detached logical thinking. What I had to do was to step back and see if I could provide some solid logic so that he would get beyond this potential deal breaker(while I was talking myself off the ledge as well).

It went something like this. Bill, remember in the memorandum we made all of those adjustments to remove owner perks from your financials and applied those adjustments to increase your EBITDA. Well those were very powerful because the buyer looked at those expenses as being eliminated after he owned the company and when he applied his 5X multiple your adjusted EBITDA, it resulted in an increase in your sales price of 5 times your eliminated expenses. Now if you want the buyer to incur those expenses once he owns the company, will you be happy with an adjusted purchase price reduced by 5 X those expenses? Believe me, you are much better off with multiplying the perks by 5 and receiving that bump in transaction value.

It was beautiful, logical, insightful, but at the end of the day, his partner convinced him to take the deal.

Well, at least I have another article, a little more wisdom, a couple of more gray hairs, and can prevent this from happening on the next deal.

6.7 – Mergers & Acquisitions Process

ENGAGEMENT AGREEMENT

The first step is the execution of the Engagement Agreement. It spells out the activities YOUR M&A ADVISOR will perform and details the fee structure. The key elements of the agreement are monthly fees, success fees, cash at close, and cancellation.

SELLER SITUATION ANALYSIS

As Steven Covey would say, "Begin with the end in mind." It is important that seller and investment banker have a meeting of the minds about the Seller's desired outcomes. We will discuss valuation expectations, deal structure (i.e. cash at close, seller financing, earn-outs, etc.) seller's post sale stay-on period and what capacity he/she desires (full time for 3 months followed by 20 hours a week for 6 months, for example)

CREATE NDA (NON-DISCLOSURE AGREEMENT), BLIND PROFILE AND APPROVAL LIST

We have a philosophy that it is to the seller's great advantage to get the sales process completed as soon as possible and that is how we operate. Our objective is to have the Blind Profile (a 2 page document that describes the company and the strategic opportunity created through the acquisition without revealing the identity of the seller) completed within the first week. The NDA is a standard document that we customize by adding the client number, i.e. Client # 060524. That number is used with prospective buyers until the NDA's are executed.

PREPARE ACQUISITION TARGET MEMORANDUM (ATM)

This is an area where our procedure differs from most in our profession. Through experience we have learned that it can be a drawn out period to get all the company information necessary to complete this document to ours and our seller's satisfaction. Some of the competitors do no marketing of the company before all the I's are dotted and the T's are crossed on this document. That could be 4 months! We believe that our client should not be paying a monthly fee to an M&A firm waiting for information. We process in parallel. We immediately produce the blind profile and begin the contact process while we are preparing the ATM. There is no better motivator than 5 executed NDA's with potential buyers to get the seller to provide the necessary information to complete the document.

PROFESSIONAL M&A MARKETING

Our process is the most effective in compressing the time period between start and closing. It is a direct sales approach that involves phone calls to each of the buyer prospects. It is very labor intensive, requiring on average 10 dials for every successful contact. When we reach the target, we have less than one minute to articulate the opportunity and get their attention.

After all, presidents of companies are very busy men. The importance of our industry specialization is quite evident here because we speak the language.

Our credibility is established with this prospect and it increases the likelihood that he will seriously consider the opportunity. If he is interested, we ask for his email (if we don't already have it) and we email him the combined Profile/NDA. We enter a follow-up task in our contact management system for 3 days if we have not received the executed NDA. If not we are back on the phone with a friendly reminder.

Another differentiator in our process is the management of the process. We keep detailed records of every phone call, email, response, reaction, and buyer feedback. Every week we have a Status Update Meeting with our client and they are provided with the Status Update Report which details where every prospect is in the "sales" process. For example, we track every NDA executed, any prospect feedback, and alter our strategic positioning or approach to improve our future effectiveness.

PROFESSIONAL M & A NEGOTIATING

This is a critical step to have the best representation you can have. Your M&A Advisor earns their fees in this step many times over. The buyer is trying to buy your company on the most favorable terms and conditions. We are trying to move the terms and conditions in your direction. By turning over every stone and professionally presenting the opportunity to a large universe of the most appropriate buyers we can bring several interested buyers to the table. We get feedback from our seller on what aspects of the offers are most favorable to them and attempt to move our best targets to an offer that combines the best features of all the offers. This is a delicate process because if a buyer feels that he is being leveraged, he will simply withdraw from the process.

LETTER OF INTENT (LOI)

We do a great deal of our negotiating before the LOI. Generally, a LOI says that if we do our due diligence and everything checks out exactly as presented thus far, and we find no surprises, we are willing to offer this much on these terms to buy your business. It is essentially a non- binding or qualified letter of intent. The other feature is there will be a lock out period for all other buyers. In other words, in return for us spending our time and resources in the due diligence process, you can

not continue to actively market your company to other buyers for a period of 45 days. That is why we negotiate so hard before the LOI, because we are then precluded from improving the T's and C's. If the due diligence is not to their liking, they may try to improve their terms and counter offer. If that happens, we have the right to go back to the other interested parties and solicit competing bids. The only way to prevent bad buyer behavior and an attack on transaction value is to have several interested buyers ready to step in. It is our job to convey this to the LOI author.

DUE DILIGENCE

This process really has two purposes for the buyer: 1. to really understand what they are buying and 2. to try to undo all that hard negotiating we did to get the value and terms in the LOI. This process is extremely detailed and exhaustive. The buyer will most likely want to see every customer contract, sales pipeline, all employee agreements, all supplier agreements, product documentation, all accounts receivable, accounts payable, any legal issues, and they may even want to make customer satisfaction phone calls (disguised for a different purpose). If anything was presented prior to due diligence that is found to not be true or accurate, get ready for a purchase price adjustment far greater than the value of the discrepancy or worse, they simply walk away because they have lost trust. The other thing that occurs is they will interpret their findings in the most favorable way for themselves and attempt to hack away at transaction value. Your M&A Advisor is standing guard at that door and will make certain that any reductions are legitimate.

DEFINITIVE PURCHASE AGREEMENT

If you have not sold a business before, you will be amazed at the length of this document and the incredible number of reps and warranties with requirements for accompanying detailed exhibits. Again, it is very important to have an experienced M&A firm by your side that has established their credibility with the buyer. The attorneys will do the legal work, but the business case is the purview of the buyer, his M&A team, the seller and MMC.

THE CLOSE

Well, we made it. Everyone will probably be mentally drained by this time because even if buyer and seller are behaving in a very professional and respectful manner, the process encompasses an incredible number of issues that must be addressed to both parties' satisfaction. You will need experienced cool heads during this pressure packed process. Sometimes we all sit in a big conference room at the seller's attorney's office and walk around the table and sign 20 piles of documents and sometimes we exchange documents via fax with hard copy follow-up via overnight carrier.

6.8 – ACTIVITY METRICS IN A TYPICAL SELL SIDE ENGAGEMENT

Refined List of Potential buyers - 482

Total Bulk emails sent - 2401

Individual emails sent - 830

Outbound Phone Calls to Buyers - 388

Executed Confidentiality Agreements /Memoranda distributed - 56

Buyer/Owner/Advisor Conference Calls - 26

Business Owner/Advisor telephone conversations - 90

Business Owner/Advisor email exchanges - 305

Letters of Intent Submitted - 11

Counter Proposals - 23

Business Owner/Advisor/ Attorney emails - 20

Business Owner/Advisor/ Attorney Conference Calls 5

Deal Closing - 1

Total elapsed time 6 - 8 Months

Total Advisor time 700 -1,000 Hours

6.9 – Owner's New Role After the Business Sale

When economic times are uncertain, business buyers become very cautious about a potential merger acquisition transaction. They attempt to negotiate for a lower price, but they also try to negotiate for the seller to have a significant interest in the post acquisition performance. This results in less cash at close and more of the transaction value tied to an earn out based on future sales of the acquired new division or business unit.

The buyers, especially experienced buyers, know that one of the key mistakes is to underestimate the amount of time and effort it is to institutionalize this new business. It takes a good deal of time to transfer the intellectual capital from the target company to the buying company. Converting customer loyalty to the new entity is not an automatic. Meshing corporate cultures can be problematic and good employees may leave. The owner is almost always viewed by the buyer as a critical element to the future success of the new division.

How is this reflected in the transaction? If the buyer views the owner as the center of her company's universe, owning all the customer and supplier relationships, possessing all the intellectual capital, and taking on the identity of the company, the transaction will involve a large earn out over several years. If the owner has done a good job of developing a management team and has delegated herself out of day to day operations, then the cash at close will be much greater and the earn out period will be reduced.

A great deal of a buyer's due diligence will focus on the owner's current role in the business and her role post acquisition. Forgive me for a broad generalization, but most lower mid-market businesses we have worked with have an owner that is a passionate subject matter expert that started the business almost as an afterthought. They are not necessarily skilled as CEO's and really do not enjoy the administrative duties required to run a small business. One of the reasons they are selling is to remove themselves from that grind of administrative duties.

That is a great platform to present to the buyer. The buyer usually has the infrastructure to handle that and does it much better than the target company. They are buying the smaller company in order to leverage their assets and grow at a much more rapid pace than the smaller company could grow on their own. The buyer wants to remove all the barriers for their new subject matter expert, provide her additional resources and support, and let her do what she does best – sell her product or service.

As the business seller, if you take that message to the buyer, you will find that the buyer will feel more comfortable about the risk profile of the potential acquisition and you will get more favorable terms. Unfortunately, many times the seller over communicates how tired they are and how much they want to get away from the pressure cooker environment they currently have. We have literally watched this unfold in the most unfavorable way for our sellers. When this message comes out, the earn out period gets extended and the cash at close gets reduced. The more the seller wants to get away the greater the buyer's attempts to lock her up for an extended period.

The lesson here is that if you are a smaller mid-market company and you want to receive the maximum value for your business, count on staying involved for a reasonable period of time post acquisition to insure the success of the buyer's new division. The buyer will structure the transaction so that you do have a vested interest in this success. It is acceptable to the buyer that you do not enjoy the day to day duties of being a CEO. They are counting on that because they already are performing that function. You can proactively present your vision of your new role in a way that will be received very positively. I want to be the product evangelist. I want to be the promoter at industry events, speaking engagements, blogs, and industry publications.

I want to focus on integrating the two companies and helping with the strategic plans. If you position it this way, the buyer will be more generous with the cash at close and will be less likely to try to lock you up for an extended earn out period.

CHAPTER 7

Buyer Negotiation Tactics

7.1 – Business Buyers Negotiating Tactics

If you are a business seller, one of the most challenging aspects of the sale process is listening to a potential buyer tell you why your baby is not beautiful. It is hard not to take that personally. A friend of mine is selling her condo and laughingly tells me of a buyer that came in and rolled a tennis ball across her floor to demonstrate that it is not perfectly level and that this flaw should justify a lower sale price. As I said, she laughed about it and did not get upset because she recognized it for what it was, a negotiating ploy.

Business sellers, however, have a huge emotional connection with their business. Their identity is intertwined with the business they have devoted years into building. These positioning statements by buyers often are interpreted as personal attacks or insensitive comments by someone that doesn't get it. Managing this process often is critical to maintaining a good buyer/seller relationship and creating an environment where a deal is possible.

Usually we schedule a conference call between buyer and seller after the buyer has reviewed the Offering Memorandum, Confidential Business Review, or "Book" that has been prepared for the business sale engagement. The reaction of the business seller as we debrief from such a call is often "a blow to the ego", "why didn't he get that?", "he doesn't understand our business", or even "what a moron!"

Below are some sample questions that demonstrate this approach from a buyer:

Q: Why are the co-op advertising cost so high this year? Is it all Lowes?

Q: There seems to be an unusually high level of product returns reflected on the 2014 YTD Financials. Please explain.

Q: What caused your dip in revenue in 2013?

Q: Your business seems to be concentrated in the United States. How much business is done outside the United States?

Q: Generally the unions are very restrictive on the use of outsourcing. Is that the case with your company?

Q: It looks like the majority of the business is originated by the owner. What happens if she leaves and how can we be protected?

Q: Your order lead time is 6 months. Does that cause you to lose orders?

Q: The US Auto market is in terminal decline. How do you see your future in that environment?

Q: Cost pressures have reduced loyalty with your Big 3 captive customers. What effect is that having on margins?

Q: Your company appears to have little or no relationships/Brand identity in China limiting potential in a very large growth market. Can you comment on this?

Q: Your licensing revenue accounted for close to $1 million in 2013. Are all of those licensing agreements expiring?

These questions are meant to help the potential

buyer really understand the seller's business and understand any issues that could impact the business in the future. The second not so subtle message is that we really understand the flaws in your company and we are going to manage your expectations and justify our less than generous offer.

That is OK. Do they expect us to take this lying down? Two can play at that game, or whatever cliché we can think of. But, we must counter punch and our defense generally takes the form of answers that either explain why a negative was a one-time occurrence or something we have already identified and have taken corrective action. Our second major counter to the negatives from the buyer is to demonstrate that we understand why they are an interested buyer in the first place and try to position our company as a strategic acquisition.

Below is a sample communication back to the buyer after a conference call in which the buyer exercised his right to try to drive down our selling price:

Subject: Thanks for the Great Questions on the Conference Call:

Bill:

Thanks to you, Jim and Brad for some very good Q&A.

As our seller and I debriefed on the call we had a couple of observations:

1. Your team was obviously very sensitive to the big box retailers pricing pressure through your own personal experience. The XYZ Product is in a different stage of its product cycle then probably most of your line that is more mature. As you know and as XYZ Company is experiencing, their marketing costs in the start-up and growth mode may be out of line with the expectations of a more mature product line.

2. We understand that the big box retailers try to turn every product into a commodity and exert pricing pressure on their suppliers accordingly. This product line seems to have enough uniqueness that it is able to avoid that commodity label. It seems to be more strategic to the stores that carry it. They are able to get some companion product pull through - engine oil, filters, belts, spark plugs, etc. for the spring and fall tune up. It is also a product that provides that Eco Friendly Halo Effect. Buyers like solutions and if your product can be part of a solution, then buyers listen and pricing pressures are not as pronounced.

3. This product currently is the market leader in a newly revived market. Because your competition

can not provide it, you could have a new reason to approach chains that may carry Competitor A, Competitor B, Competitor C, etc. This product could be an effective door opener.

4. You correctly observed by doing more of the component production yourselves, you could substantially improve the product line margins.

5. The product could be easily integrated into your current line and current distribution systems with minor incremental costs.

This looks like it could be a "strategic acquisition" in that it can easily achieve results well beyond the sum of its parts.

We look forward to continuing your investigation and due diligence process with us. Thanks again for your efforts and your consideration.

You may be asking yourself, does this actually do any good? Well, it depends. If they have the feeling that they are the only buyer in the process and we are selling the company from a position of weakness, our counter efforts are largely ineffective. If, however, they have the impression that the aforementioned Competitor A, Competitor B, and Competitor C have been presented the same positioning and have bought into one or two of the strategic arguments, then it really does work.

We try to send back our own not so subtle message. We know what we have. We understand the market and the competition. We understand the strategic implications of you or one of your competitors in control of our product line. We have other options besides you, so you might have to alter your expectations on how much you are willing to pay to become the ultimate buyer. Plus, this helps our seller feel less like a punching bag and more like a worthy opponent.

7.2 – Business Buyers are Savvy Shoppers

The business sale process is a complex battle for leverage. A seller wants to invite many qualified buyers to the table and position his company to produce strategic value. The experienced professional business buyer has his own arsenal of tools to move the balance of power in his favor. Here we discuss how Private Equity Groups approach the process and try to stack the odds in their favor.

We preach to our business seller clients the benefits of testing the markets and inviting many qualified buyers to participate in the process. The ultimate goal is to get two or more buyers that recognize the tremendous synergies that the combined companies could realize and produce offers that are not based on a financial multiple, but on a strategic value premium. A financial multiple would be a purchase value something like 4 X EBITDA (basically cash flow) or 70% of annual revenue.

What would produce strategic value? The good news is that this can be created in a number of different ways. The evil "Wall Street stereotype" is to eliminate duplicate functions and save a tremendous amount in payroll expenses. I am not a big fan of this as the reason for doing an M&A deal. Somehow tearing something apart does not represent any particular management imagination or skill. Identifying ways to build value by creating the sum of the parts that far exceeds the inputs is real visionary management.

This strategic value can be created by acquiring a complementary product line that can be added to a strong sales and distribution network. Acquisition targets can provide superior systems, business models, product technology, and management talent that can be leveraged by the new combined company to produce revenues and profits that far exceed the two separate companies.

This sounds easy on paper and makes a lot of sense, but the truth is that most acquisitions fall short of expectations because, integrating all the systems, personnel, culture, locations, customers, etc. is complex. This makes buyers cautious. When buyers get cautious, they revert back to the conservative financial multiple which basically provides a safety net to their investment if the post acquisition synergies are not realized.

We subscribe to a private equity group database which helps us identify likely buyers of our sellers based on searching their investing criteria and identifying their portfolio companies. A surprising discovery I made is that in this particular universe of the largest 3500 private equity groups, they owned a combined 46,000 companies. If you wanted to draw any conclusions about business buyer behavior, this would be your group of target subjects.

First conclusion is these guys want to win. Sure it's money, but it is the game and the competition and thrill of the conquest that also drives these serial business acquirers. They think they are the smartest guys in the room (hey check their educational, and job history background) and on paper they may just be. But you only need to have one failed $20 million acquisition to instill some real rigor and financial conservatism into your process. They want to stack the deck to put as much as they can in their favor to make these investments winners.

The first thing they do is look for Warren Buffet type businesses. You know the ones that have a durable competitive advantage, positive cash flow, steady growth rate, loyal customers...... They want to draft Payton Manning coming out of Tennessee - Great start.

The next tenant of their success formula is to take advantage of the large company valuation premium. This is how it works. Their first acquisition into a market space is generally a bigger company, say $25 million in revenue. Let's say that this valve and pump company sells for a 6.1 X EBITDA multiple. They then attempt to make a series of tuck-in acquisitions of a $5 million valve company here and a $4 million pump company there. These smaller companies command a smaller valuation multiple than the large company, say 4 X EBITDA. The day the acquisition is completed, the PEG has already won because the acquired company is now valued at the higher EBITDA multiple of its new parent. They make a series of these investments, grow the company organically as well for 7 years and then sell their $150 million in revenue company to a strategic buyer at an EBITDA multiple of 7.8 X.

These sophisticated buyers are very disciplined in their acquisition process and very seldom stray from the strict EBITDA multiple offer. In order to stick to that discipline, they have to look at a lot of deals. We normally ask our buyers that have signed NDA's and looked at our client, and then withdrew, why they dropped out. We get a lot of different answers, but the top answer is that they were in another deal and would not be able to process both at the same time. Most of these firms invite 50 - 100 potential acquisitions into the top of the funnel for each one that they complete.

So, what they are doing is creating the counter-balance of the leverage we are trying to create by getting lots of potential buyers involved. They have multiple options, so if the price gets too high, they go for easier prey. If the sellers are difficult, they move on. If the financial reporting is shaky and unclear they find a company where it is transparent.

Please don't let me give you the impression that this process is totally by the numbers. There are great companies that will command a premium, but just like buying a luxury automobile, they are still shopping.

7.3 – Business Buyers are Valuation Experts

As it turns out, buyers are astute business valuation analysts. They look for certain features when they assess the desirability of a business acquisition. Private equity groups are particularly rigorous in this process. Without exaggeration, we receive at least five contacts per week from private equity groups describing their buying criteria. The most surprising statement contained in a majority of these solicitations is the statement, "We are pretty much industry agnostic."

They may add in a couple qualifiers like we avoid information technology firms, start-ups and turn- arounds. Below is a typical description:

Example Capital Group seeks to acquire established businesses that have stable, positive cash flows and EBITDA between $2mm and $7mm. We will consider investments that satisfy a majority of the following characteristics:

Financial
Revenues between $10mm and $50 mm

EBITDA between $2mm and $7mm

Operating margins greater than 15%

Management

Owners or senior management willing to transition out of daily operations

Experienced second tier management team willing to remain with the company

Business

Long term growth potential

Large and fragmented market

Recurring revenue business model

History of profitability and cash flow

Medium to low technology

I chuckle when I get these. You and 5,000 other private equity firms are looking for the same thing. It is like saying I am looking for a college quarterback that looks like Peyton Manning. Pretty good chance that he will be successful in his transition to the pros. That is exactly what the buyer is looking for – pretty good chance that this acquisition will be successful once we buy it. Just give me a business that looks like the one above and even I would look good running it.

On the other hand, more often than not we are representing seller clients that do not look nearly this good. Getting buyer feedback on why our client is not an attractive acquisition candidate is often a painful process, but can be quite instructive. Unfortunately it is usually too late to make the needed changes during the current M&A process. Many businesses are great lifestyle businesses for the owners, but do not translate into an attractive acquisition for the potential buyer because the business model is not easily transferable and scalable.

In these businesses the value the owner can extract is greater by just holding on and running it a few more years that he can realize in an outright sale. What are these characteristics that reduce the salability of a business or diminish its value in the eyes of a potential buyer? Below are our top 5 value destroyers:

1. The business is too transactional in nature. What this means is that too much of the company's revenues are dependent on new sales as opposed to long term contracts. Contractually recurring revenue is much more valuable than what might be called historically recurring revenue.

2. Too much of the business is concentrated

within the owners. Account relationships, intellectual property, supplier relationships and the business identity are all at fish when the business changes hands and the owners cash out and walk out the door.

3. Too much of the business is concentrated in too few customers. Customer concentration poses a high risk for a new owner because the loss of one or two accounts could turn the buyer's investment sour in a big hurry. The buyer fears that all accounts are vulnerable with the change in ownership.

4. Little competitive differentiation. Buyers are just not attracted to businesses with no identifiable competitive advantage. A commodity product or service is too difficult to defend and margins and profits will continually be challenged by the market.

5. The market segment is too narrow, has too little potential, or is shrinking. If your market place is so narrow that even if your company had 100% market penetration and you sales were capped at $20 million, a larger company would not get very excited about an acquisition because you could not move their needle.

A business owner that is contemplating the sale

of his business could greatly benefit from this rigorous buyer feedback two of three years prior to actually beginning the business sale process. A valuable exercise to take business owners through is a simulated buyer review. During this process we help identify those areas that could detract from the business selling price or the amount of cash he receives at closing.

This process is certainly less painful than when we were negotiating a letter of intent with a buyer from Dallas and he said to our client, "Brother, your overhead expenses are 20% too high for this sales level." Another buyer in another client negotiation said, "I can't pay you a lot in cash at closing when your assets walk out the door every night. It will have to be mostly future earn out payments."

As a business owner you can both identify and fix your company's value detractors prior to your sale or you can let the new owner correct them and keep all that value himself. Viewing your business as a buyer would well in advance of your business sale and then correcting those weaknesses will result in a higher sales price and a greater percentage of your transaction value in cash at closing.

7.4 – In a Business Sale the Process Favors the Buyer

Unless your company is one of those must have, breakthrough, technology companies with buyers crawling all over you, you are subject to a process that greatly favors the business buyer. This presentation will identify these attacks on transaction value and approaches you can use to hold your ground against this formidable opponent. It may be helpful to look at it like a fencing match; buyer thrust, seller parry.

Thrust - Buyer experience. If the buyer is a private equity group, they buy companies for a living. They will have acquired dozens of companies prior to entering the competition for your business. If it is an industry buyer, they likely have an individual or department whose sole function is to look for business acquisitions. For most business sellers this is their first and only rodeo. What you don't know will definitely hurt you, or at least cost you.

Parry - Do not go it alone. Hire an experienced M&A advisor to help you, not only for the packaging and marketing of your company, but for defending the value you thought you were going to receive at closing. Make sure you get an experienced deal attorney at the contract stage to counter act the incredibly one-sided agreement that the buyer's team will present.

Thrust - Buyer choices. I know this will come as a shock, but yours is not the only business the buyer is seriously evaluating for acquisition. For private equity buyers, they generally look at about 100 companies for each one they buy. They will have several deals in the queue along with yours to give them plenty of options, to leverage one against the others, and to reduce emotional attachment to any one deal.

Parry - Seller choices. If the seller tries to sell his company on his own, he can usually only process one buyer at a time in a serial process because of all his other duties running the company. If a buyer knows he is the only buyer, count on bad behavior - inability to tie him down on a firm offer, missed time commitments, delays, endless information requests, and on and on. If, however you have been able to attract multiple buyers, your negotiating position is strengthened and you can offset these buyer tactics.

Thrust - Buyer controlling the negotiating dialogue. It is not uncommon to hear something like this from an experienced buyer, "Well last year you had a spike in profitability, I am just going to use the average of the last three years as the basis for my offer."

Parry- Seller response via Advisor. It makes no sense to try to negotiate at this level. We just say, "Feel free to slice it any way that works for you. At the end of the day, if that approach makes your offer not competitive, you will eliminate yourself from the competition."

Thrust - Buyer getting you off the market with a loosely worded LOI that allows him to "interpret the terms" in his favor deep into the due diligence process.

Parry - Seller not counter signing the LOI until terms are defined. There are several key terms of the LOI, so we will give each one their own Thrust and Parry.

Thrust - Buyer attempted treatment of Working Capital. Most buyers attempt initial language for Working Capital in the LOI that looks something like this: Working Capital Adjustment: There shall be a typical working capital adjustment to accommodate for changes to the working capital balance, (including cash. accounts receivable and accounts payable) as of the day of closing. During due diligence the Purchaser will set a working capital target by determining a normal and customary level of current assets including a positive cash balance. There shall be sufficient working capital, including a cash balance which shall be sufficient to operate the business on an ongoing day to today basis and the buyer will not need to fund working capital simply to operate the business immediately after the transaction.

Parry - Not so fast Zorro! This seems like a perfectly reasonable treatment and unfortunately many unsuspecting sellers will counter sign an LOI with this language in place. The result of this is either he is going to get taken to the cleaners on the level the buyer decides on, deep into the due diligence process, or the seller will blow up the deal deep into the process. Neither a good result and the sad part is that it could easily be prevented. The first rule of LOI's is do not take your company off the market with a very important term not defined up front. This language enables their team of experts to calculate their own opinion of "reasonable and customary" while you have no negotiating leverage. You have already taken your company off the market as a buyer requirement to enable due diligence with a no shop clause.

The second very important mistake is that by leaving that term undefined, you have not really benchmarked the proposed transaction value against other bids. We had a client that kept a net working capital surplus far greater than what was normally required to run the business. Let's say that they kept a surplus of $400,000 when their normal monthly business expenses were $100,000. So the level could be set as a surplus of $100,000. Now the buyers bring in their experts and look at your last 12 months' balance sheets and proclaim that your historical level of $400,000 is what they need, then you may have just sacrificed $300,000 of transaction value. If you have one buyer that bids $3,000,000 for your company with a net working capital surplus requirement of $100,000 and you close with $400,000 surplus, $300,000 is returned to you as transaction value. This makes the total transaction value $3,300,000.

If the undefined working capital surplus buyer bids $3,100,000 and calculates, after the LOI, that his requirement is $400,000, then his transaction value is short the other bid by $200,000!

This can all be prevented by the seller insisting that the LOI include a net working capital level commitment with the calculation methodology spelled out. Each buyer may have their own opinion of what that number should be, but this exercise will allow you to equalize the bids and determine which one is truly superior. Unfortunately, the buyers try to leave this vague in their LOI so that ninety days into the due diligence process they render their buyer favorable opinion and count on the seller suffering from deal fatigue and just caving in on this meaningful loss in value. The buyers know that they do damage to your future chances if you put your company back on the market with the stigma of the previous deal blowing up during due diligence. It usually results in a market discount being applied to your company the second time around.

Thrust - An earnout clause with punitive "all or none" language. In the realm of SMB mergers and acquisitions, an earnout is a common practice and a perfectly reasonable component of a business sale transaction. It is often an effective way to bridge the valuation gap between buyer and seller and to align the interests of buyer and seller for post acquisition business performance. But like other components here, there is good earnout language and there is earnout language that is one-sided in favor of the buyer. An example of earnout language from a buyer LOI is: The total earnout shall be paid over three years. The total possible payout amount $1.5 million based on growing EBITDA by 5% per year over last year's rate of $1,250,000.

The target EBITDA in year one is $1,312,500, year 2 is $1,378,125, and year 3 is $1,447,031. If the target is hit, the payout will be $500,000 for the year. If the achievement is between 85% - 99% of target, the payout will be that percentage attainment X $500,000. If the attainment is less than 85% of target, no earnout payment will be made.

Parry - In general we recommend that earnouts be based on a number that cannot be easily manipulated by the buying company. So measures like net profit and EBITDA are less favorable. Here they can insert some expense items like "corporate overhead" which are out of your control. We prefer tying earnouts to measures such as total sales or Gross Profit Margin; far more difficult to leave up to interpretation. Next, we never recommend an all or nothing earnout clause. Normally earnouts are a meaningful percentage of the overall transaction value and if an unforeseen event takes you below their cut-off target, you have sacrificed some serious value. Our argument is that if there is a big short-fall, the % of that shortfall in their earnout payment is enough to keep buyer and seller interests aligned post acquisition.

If there is a downside adjustment in the earnout calculation (there always is) then we like to have the corresponding upside for surpassing target performance. In other words, if you miss your target by 10% than you only receive 90% of that year's earnout payment target. If you hit 110% of your target, your earnout payment should be 110% of that target.

We also recommend that the earnout be formula driven and include an example calculation as shown here. The earnout would total $1,500,000 and be paid in the first three years after the closing within 30 days of the anniversary date. The earnout would be based on the trailing twelve months revenues and a target to grow those revenues by 5% per year over the first 3 years following closing. So the target for year one (again using the prior year end as the example) would be $5,000,000 X 1.05 = $5,250,000. For year 2 another 5% growth would result in a target of $5,512,500. And for year 3 another 5%

growth would result in a target of $5,788,125, for a three year total of $15,550,625. Dividing this by the total earnout payment at target ($1,500,000) results in an earnout payment of 9.06% of revenues for the first three years. The payment would be made annually within 30 days of closing of the company's books for 12, 24, and 36 months following closing.

For each year's earnout payment, the actual payout amount would be the calculated by applying the Payout percentage rate of 9.06% times the actual revenues. As an example, if the revenue for year three came in at $5,000,000 that would be multiplied by 9.06% and result in an earnout payment of $453,000. If the year three revenues came in at $6,000,000, the earnout payment would be $546,600.

Great, we have handled each thrust with our skillful parry. Match over, right? Keep that face protector on, the match is just heating up.

Thrust - the due diligence surprise. We noticed that your average billing per customer is smaller than our average billing rate, we are going to have to adjust our value.

Parry - What about the memorandum, the detailed customer lists, the monthly billing report that you reviewed prior to executing the LOI didn't you understand? Our price is firm. If you want to adjust, we are cancelling the LOI and we are back on the market.

Thrust - we noticed that you had a spike in this particular type of revenue which is unusually profitable. We do not believe that this is sustainable and are going to have to adjust our bid to account for that.

Parry - If you analyze it correctly, last year was pretty much the norm for this type of revenue. The year prior was actually the outlier and much lower than average. Secondly, if you truly allocated corporate overhead to this income category, you would find it about the same level of profitability as our other lines of business. No adjustment is warranted.

OK - we held our own during that round. Now it is just a formality to get the purchase agreements signed and provide our wire transfer instructions. Not yet, pick up your sword.

Thrust - You receive the definitive purchase agreement from the buyer's attorney and it looks like you have to rep and warranty your first born in order to get the deal signed. All of a sudden you see escrows and holdbacks, and guarantees that were not mentioned in the LOI. Much of that is pretty standard stuff although it will be very slanted to the benefit of the buyer.

Parry- no material changes to the deal economics allowed. We signed the LOI and provided you a no shop in order to allow you to perform due diligence. We were very detailed in our LOI in order to compare your bid with others that were very close. Without any legitimate finding of mis information in the due diligence process, the economics remain the same.

As for the scary reps and warranties, hold backs and escrows we let our lawyers talk with their lawyers. It is almost like they have the lawyers secret pinky handshake and they carve through this language with clarity and precision. What it usually boils down to is what is reasonable and customary in transactions that are similar to this one. If there are any remaining issues they identify them and ask the seller and his advisor to work them out with the buyer. By this stage, these final points are settled constructively.

Thrust - Oh, just one more thing, you are going to throw in the floor mats and the undercoating at no charge. We tell our clients to expect this because it is just the nature of the buyers. Here is how it is manifested in a business sale transaction. The closing date is set for September 30th, month end. We want to move the closing date back to October 7 so we can take a look at your month end numbers. Do you have any concerns? No we just want to make sure things are on track.

Parry - Not much we can do about this one but try to anticipate what they may be looking at for that final attack on value and to prepare our counter attack. This one is a little trickier, however, because in prior attacks we had the luxury of time in order to strategize and craft our response. This one is usually real time where emotions are on the jagged edge. We ask our client to prepare a response to our anticipated last minute objection and then we, as their advisors, take the first attack. We want to have the client stay above the fray and preserve their relationship for the upcoming partnership together. If that effort is not accepted and the buyer insists on an adjustment based on "it looks like you are not tracking to hit your first year earnout target." We prepare the seller with, "You know that we put in the earnout in order to align your interests with ours going forward. I have a good deal of transaction value tied to hitting our targets and I would not have signed this agreement unless I was fully confident that I would collect every dollar of that earnout."

Unfortunately, in spite of my best efforts I view a stalemate as the best outcome we can hope for once we are off the market. As you can see the leverage totally shifts to the buyer. The price is never increased during due diligence and contract negotiation. There is pressure to even keep the business flat during this process because a good deal of the owner's attention and emotions are going to be focused on the process of selling his business as opposed to just running his business. So our process is to make it evident that there are several qualified buyers that are very close in their offers to the winning offer. If there is buyer bad behavior we can simply plug in the next best bidder. The other major strategy we employ is to be very detailed, formula and example driven in the LOI that we recommend our client execute.

CHAPTER 8

Due Diligence

8.1 – FAQ's From Business Buyers

An area of great concern to our business selling clients as we help prepare them for a buyer visit is what questions the buyer is likely to ask. Below are a representative set of questions that we have encountered. We will not provide you with the answers because they will vary with each business seller. However, we will provide a buyer motivation framework so that you can answer the questions with this common framework in mind.

Buyers want to eliminate as much risk as possible because an acquisition, by its very nature is a risky business decision. A buyer does not want to discover or be confronted with a bunch of Gotcha's after the check has cleared. As a seller, you must never convey the attitude of this place is falling apart and you can't wait to dump this dog. Your reasons for selling are very important and should focus on estate planning considerations, retirement and diversifying my assets or my favorite, we just do not have the resources to take advantage of all the market potential that we have created.

Another theme is that you want to convey how strong your staff is. You want to portray how the account relationships are managed by multiple staff members. You need to communicate just how widespread the intellectual property is dispersed among the staff. The owner has an easy job because the employees handle all of that.

Future potential and momentum are important. Make sure you can articulate the opportunities for growth that you have identified, and are either pursuing now or are planning to pursue if you had more resources. So keeping these themes in mind, be prepared to answer many of the following:

Why are you selling your business?

What are the last three year's net operating profits?

Who are your biggest competitors?

What are your industry ratios and trends?

What do you think I can do to increase sales and profits?

Why are you not doing that to increase sales and profits?

Will you hold financing for the purchase of the business?

Will you be willing to stay with the business for a period of time after the sale?

Will you agree to a covenant not to compete?

Will the business sale include the transfer of real estate?

Don't you have children to transfer your business to?

Do you want a corporate stock sale or asset sale?

Who knows that the business is for sale?

Who will I be negotiating with?

What is your timetable for completing the business sale?

What do you do everyday?

Do you anticipate any problems with me getting credit from your suppliers

Do any of your suppliers represent more than 10% of your purchases? If yes, who are they?

What is it that you like best and least about the business?

What do you believe is the profile of the ideal buyer for this business?

What can be done to build the business?

How long will it take me to really learn this business?

How long can I count on you to train me after the sale?

What keeps you up at night about the business?

What are the details of the lease? How long? Any options? Do you anticipate any problems with the landlord assigning it to me or entering into a new lease?

How much vacation do you take (not that you're looking for time off...rather, you want to know if they have adequate staff that will allow you time away)?

Are you the only owner?

Who are the employees? Any manager in place? Are there any employees that are critical to the business?

Are you willing to finance part of the purchase? If not, why?

Net revenue seemed to experience a huge

decline last year versus previous years. What happened?

How much of the revenue is the owner responsible for?

How much of the revenue are the other business development people responsible for?

What are the titles and responsibilities of each of the employees? Please state how long each has been with the company and what they are being paid, and how they are being paid. If they have success-based compensation please let me know the actual for the past three years for each person.

What are their revenue production goals? Other goals?

What does their five-year plan look like going forward?

Why is the owner selling the business?

Can I see actual P&L statement for the last five years?

Is there one person in house today that would be interested in and capable of running the day-to-day operation while keeping up personal production and receiving an override and perhaps equity stake in the business?

Is the owner open to an acquisition plan that

would be tied into continued success of the firm over the next five years?

Do the employees have non-compete agreements with the company? If so what is the nature of the non-compete? If not, why not?

Is the current owner willing to sign a non-compete agreement as part of the acquisition?

What is the owner's salary, bonus, fees, and commissions on an annual basis and over the last five years?

How much of the business are we likely to lose if the current owner retires or discontinues affiliation with the company? How would the owner propose to mitigate the loss for a new owner?

This list is by no means exhaustive and there may be questions that arise that are unique to your particular business or industry. However, if you can answer these questions with an awareness of the buyer's risk mitigation approach, your firm will be viewed as a better acquisition target. We are in no way suggesting that your answers are not truthful, we are just suggesting that you surround them with an attractive packaging. Any answers that are found to be inaccurate during the due diligence process will result in punitive adjustments to purchase value.

If you remember the old interview question, "What would you say is the biggest negative about your business approach?" Your positive answer was something like, "Well, I am so driven to be successful that I am sometimes impatient with people that do not share my same drive or capability." That's how we are suggesting you approach this. So for example, you have lost a few deals to XYZ Big Company. How will that impact the business going forward? Well, the competition from the XYZ Company is a good news bad news situation. The bad news is that they are a very tough competitor, but the good news is their attention to our space reinforces our view of the long term potential. How's that for positive?

8.2 – Get a Letter of Intent Prior to Going Through Due Diligence

Due diligence is an exhaustive exercise with a great deal of resource from both the buyer and the seller invested in the process. Not only is it a large resource drain, but the buyer learns all of your company's secrets including strategy, pricing, customers, suppliers and other important proprietary information. Why would you go through this process without understanding the terms and conditions of your potential sale to the buyer once that process is completed?

The purpose of a letter of intent is to define the economic terms and conditions that apply to the pending business sale if the due diligence results in no material differences in the condition of the seller's business. In simple terms, it means that if I go over your books and records in great detail and I verify that everything you had previously presented checks out, I am willing to pay you X dollars for your business under the set of Y terms. Below is a sample Letter of Intent.

Mr. X. X. Last Name

Address 1

Address 2

City, ST Zip

PERSONAL & CONFIDENTIAL

Re: Purchase of Assets of ABC Corp.

Dear Mr. Last Name:

The purpose of this letter is to set forth the general terms and conditions of the proposed purchase by NEWCO, a corporation ("Buyer") of substantially all of the assets of ABC Corp., an Illinois corporation ("Seller").

1. Purchase and Sale of Assets. At the Closing

(as hereinafter defined), Buyer will purchase all of the assets including accounts receivable but not cash on hand and rights of Seller, including all real and personal property, contract rights, patents and intellectual property. All of the assets to be purchased are referred to below as the "Purchased Assets."

2. Liabilities. Buyer will assume no liabilities of Seller except the following ("Assumed Liabilities"):

The obligations of Seller arising under purchase orders from the Seller's customers in the ordinary course of business, sales orders issued to Seller's suppliers in the ordinary course of business, leases of personal property.

3. Purchase Price. As consideration for the Purchased Assets, Buyer will assume the Assumed Liabilities and will pay to Seller the amount equal to the following: _____ ($_____) dollars (the "Purchase Price").

Payment is to be made as follows: $ _____ in cash at the Closing, and the remainder by delivery of the Buyer's promissory note in the principal amount of _____

The _____-year _____ interest bearing note at the Prime Rate on the date of Closing will be issued by BUYER with interest paid quarterly and principal paid as a balloon payment at the end of the seven year term.

Employment Contract. Buyer and Seller will enter into an employment agreement which will provide for employment as Consultant and provide Seller with an annual salary of _____ and such other normal fringe benefits as shall be mutually agreed upon and set forth in the employment agreement. In addition to the base annual salary, Seller will receive ___% commission on sales in excess of $ _____. The employment agreement will be for a three-year term. Basis of commissions shall be mutually agreed upon.

Recognizing that Mr. Last Name is a valuable resource to the well being of the ongoing business of SELLER, BUYER expects his daily cooperation as part of the total purchase price for at least the first six months after the closing. The employment agreement will require a minimum of _____ days and a maximum of _____ days per year.

4. Conditions. The purchase and sale of the Purchased Assets contemplated by this letter of intent will be subject to terms and conditions customary to transactions of the type, including, without limitation, the following:

No change occurring prior to the Closing which materially and adversely affects the Business, Purchased Assets, financial condition, and prospects of Seller; Completion of Buyer's examination of the financial condition, properties and business of Seller which examination shall not have revealed the existence of any fact, matter or circumstance which in Buyer's judgment could materially and adversely affect the Business;

Buyer obtaining financing for the purchase of Purchased Assets at terms which are acceptable to the buyer; and

Both parties agree to a Definitive Purchase Agreement.

5. Complete Access. Following the acceptance of the letter of intent by the Seller until the Closing, Seller will give to Buyer and its representatives complete access to all of its books, records, financial statements and other documents and materials relating to the Business and to Seller's customers and suppliers.

6. Confidentiality. The information furnished by Seller to Buyer and its employees, advisors and consultants pursuant to Section 6 shall be subject to the provisions of the confidentiality agreement. Until

the Closing, Buyer will at all times hold and cause its employees, advisors, and consultants to hold in strict confidence all confidential documents and information concerning Seller which have been or will be furnished by Seller to Buyer or its employees, advisors and consultants in connection with the transactions contemplated by this letter of intent.

If the transactions contemplated by this letter of intent are not consummated, regardless of the reason therefore, such as confidence will be maintained by Buyer, except to the extent such information (a) was previously known to Buyer prior to disclosure by Seller, (b) is in the public domain through no fault of Buyer, (c) is acquired by Buyer from a third party not known by Buyer to be under an obligation of confidence to Seller, or (d) is required by law or legal process to be disclosed.

Such documents and information will not be used to the detriment of Seller or otherwise in any other manner and all documents, materials and other written information provided by Seller to Buyer, including all copies and extracts thereof, will be returned to Seller immediately upon its written request.

7. Expenses. Buyer and Seller will be responsible

for the payment of their respective expenses and professional fees incurring in connection with the negotiation an consummation of the transactions contemplated by this letter of intent, except as may be otherwise provided in the Purchase Agreement (as defined below).

8. No Other Negotiations; Brokers. Seller acknowledges that Buyer has incurred and will incur significant costs in reviewing and analyzing Seller's business and proceeding in good faith to purchase the Purchased Assets as described herein.

Therefore, for a period of _____ (___) days commencing on the date of Seller's acceptance of this letter of intent unless Buyer notifies Seller in writing that negotiations in respect to the trans-actions contemplated hereby have terminated, nei-ther Seller nor it shareholders will directly or indirectly solicit or make or entertain any offer or proposal from or to a third party regarding the sale or possible sale of Purchased Assets or a sale of the stock of Seller or discuss in any manner any such sale with any third party or provide any information concerning the Purchased Assets to any third par-ty.

In the event that Seller or any shareholder

receives any inquiry from a third party with respect to such a sale or possible sale, Seller will notify Buyer and inform such a party of Seller's obligations under Section 8. It is understood that XYZ Merger Group, Inc. has acted as broker on behalf of Buyer and that Buyer shall be responsible for the payment of any and all fees and expenses due to such a firm.

9. Closing. It is anticipated that the closing of the transactions contemplated by this letter of intent (the "Closing") will occur _____ (__) days following the date of execution of the Purchase Agreement, but in no event later than _____.

10. Public Announcement. The parties will make a joint public announcement transactions described herein, with the content and timing of such an announcement to be mutually agreed upon by parties. Each party will consult with the other party prior to issuing any press release or otherwise making any public statement with respect to the transactions contemplated by this letter of intent and will not issue any such release or make any such statement over the reasonable objection of the other party, except as required by law.

The parties will proceed diligently to negotiate

in good faith towards the preparation and execution of a definitive agreement (the "Purchase Agreement") containing the agreed-upon terms and conditions as well as the customary warranties, representations, covenants, and indemnifications normally associated with the purchase and sale of assets. It is understood that except for the provisions of Sections 6, 7, 8 and 10, this letter of intent is not legally binding on either Buyer or Seller, but that it is intended only to evidence the good faith intent of the Buyer and Seller to proceed toward the transactions contemplated hereby, subject to the negotiation of certain terms and conditions not dealt with herein.

If the terms set forth in this letter meet with your approval, please indicate your acceptance by signing both copies of this letter and returning one to the undersigned. Upon the return of an executed copy of this letter, we will instruct our attorneys to proceed with the preparation of the Purchase Agreement and related documents. Our offer to enter into this letter of intent will remain open until the close of business on _____.

Very truly yours,

_____

Agreed to and accepted on this _____ day of
_____, 20_____.

By:_____

Its_____

The Letter of Intent is non-binding so that if the buyer discovers some surprises, he can walk away with no penalty or he can attempt to renegotiate the previously stated terms and conditions. The seller should do his negotiating or have his advisor do the negotiating prior to counter signing the LOI because a smart buyer will try to lock you up for a period of 45 to 90 days while he performs his due diligence. This lock up means that you are not allowed to invite any other bidders into the mix until the period expires or until either party has cancelled the LOI. Once the due diligence is completed, then the deal is memorialized by a much more detailed definitive purchase agreement.

8.3 – Prepare for the Buyer Visit

In a business sale, a very important event prior to receiving letters of intent is the buyer visit. Don't be fooled into thinking that this is a simple headquarters tour. Experienced buyers know just the right questions to ask to uncover risks and to discover opportunities. We try to coach our sellers on how to present and how to answer these carefully scripted questions.

Unfortunately, a man or a woman that has called their own shots for the last 25 years is not always receptive to coaching. If we get a feeling that our advice is falling on deaf ears, we schedule the first visit with a buyer that is not the top candidate. Once our seller has made a few tactical errors in this dry run, they are then open to some coaching.

This is what we tell them. Acquiring another company is very risky. Mistakes can damage the buying company. Therefore, a buyer is looking to identify and mitigate risks. Their questioning will focus on what they can expect once they are the owner of your business. Are you bailing on a business that is on a downward spiral? When you leave, will major customers leave with you? Will your key employees stay? Will our company have your strong support in transitioning your knowledge and intellectual capital to our staff?

The number one question is, why are you selling your business? The unacceptable answer is, so I can get away as quickly as possible and sip umbrella drinks on an island. The correct positioning of your exit is, we have built this business and are nearing retirement. In order to realize the future potential we will have to invest back into it at a time when we should be diversifying our assets. A strategic larger company could leverage our assets to achieve much greater market penetration than we could.

Another important theme is that you are in control. You understand your costs and your margins. You can identify the opportunities for growth that a better capitalized company could capture. You can articulate your strengths. You know your weaknesses and they are simply that you do not have enough resources, capital, or distribution to capitalize on all this potential you have created. You understand your market and your competition.

Buyers like to believe they are buying a business at a discount. You should try to present your weaknesses in such a way that the buyer will think, we can easily correct that. For example, an eight week order backlog could be considered a negative. A smart buyer will think, that is a high class problem. I wonder how many orders they lose because of the order delay? We could hire three more people, open two more work bays and cut that backlog down to ten days, immediately capturing 10% greater sales.

Another example is that the selling company is technology focused and really lacks sales and marketing expertise. The savvy buyer with a fully developed sales and marketing engine pictures a 20% increase in sales immediately. If the selling company already had these weaknesses corrected, the buyer would certainly have to reflect that in the purchase price. Because the weaknesses exist and the buyer has already identified how his company will correct them, he views it as buying potential at a discount.

A corporate visit should be a good two-way exchange of information. The seller should ask such things as: How long have you been in business? How many locations do you have? How many employees work for your company? This question is a good way to back into company revenues by applying industry metrics of revenue per employee. Sometimes private companies are hesitant to reveal sales figures. The seller wants to determine whether the buyer is big enough to make the acquisition.

What are your biggest challenges? Who are your biggest competitors? How do you see the market? Where are your best opportunities? Have you made any prior acquisitions? How do you feel about them? What are you really good at? What areas would you like to improve? How would you see integrating our company with yours?

There is some very important information that you are seeking from this line of questioning. First, their answers give you some hooks on which to hang the assets of your company in order to drive up your perceived value to the buyer. Find their opportunities and show how your company combined with theirs can help capture them. Show how your assets will give them an advantage over their competitors. Show how your combined assets can eliminate some of their problems or weaknesses.

You want to determine if there is a cultural and a philosophical fit. Is there trust? Do you feel comfortable? Do they "get it" in terms of recognizing your company's strategic value or are they just trying to buy your company at some rule of thumb financial multiple?

Often a company acquisition is comprised of cash at close and some form of deferred transaction value like an earn out. If your deal was structured like this, do you have confidence that you would reach your maximum in future payments? Have they been able to articulate their growth plan after they acquire you?

As you can see, the buyer visit should not be looked at as simply a show and tell corporate visit. It should be viewed as an opportunity for the seller to gather valuable information that will help him answer three questions: 1. Is it a fit? 2. How can my company help them grow and better compete? 3. Are they willing and able to pay me for that?

8.4 – A Technique to Improve Business Selling Price During Due Diligence

One of the things I like best about representing small business owners as an M&A Advisor is that no two days are the same. Yes, deals have common elements, but it is those unique details at the margin that must be handled on the fly that can mean the difference between success and failure. To prepare our clients for those 80% deal elements in common we have written articles on each stage of the process and we review those articles with our client prior to the stage. So for example we will review the most commonly asked questions from buyers on conference calls and we will role play with our clients on answering these questions.

If the client knows what to expect prior to the stage, any bump in the road does not turn into a deal threatening event. We try to manage and control what we can, but more often than not something new surfaces that is new to our experience. How those surprises are handled often can be the difference between closing and the deal blowing up. In a recent transaction that we completed, we had one of those first time surprises. Luckily we were able to get past it and improve our preparation for the next deal and as an added bonus, resulted in this article.

Due diligence was coming to a satisfactory close and the definitive purchase agreements, seller notes, and employment contracts were moving through the process without a hitch. We were set to close on April 30 and ten days prior to closing the buyer said, we just want to see your closing numbers through April, so let's move the closing back 5 days. What were we going to do tell them no? I said, well you have already completed due diligence, are you concerned about the April numbers? He said, no, we just want to make sure everything is on track.

My radar went off and I thought about all of the events external to our deal that could cause the deal not to close. How many deals failed to close, for example, that were on the table during the stock market crash of 1987? The second part of my radar

said that we needed to be prepared to defend transaction value one final time. I suggested he bring in
his outside accountant to help us analyze such things
as sales versus projections, gross margins, deal pipeline,
revenue run rate, etc. We were going to be prepared.
We knew that if things looked worse, the buyer was
going to request an adjustment.

Now here comes the surprise. The outside
accountant discovered that there was a revenue
recognition issue and our client had actually under-
stated profitability by a meaningful amount. This
was discovered after the originally scheduled closing date and it meant that the buyer had based his
purchase price on an EBITDA number that was too
low. Easy deal, right? We just take his transaction
value for the original deal and the EBITDA number he used and calculated an EBITDA multiple.
We then applied that multiple to our new EBITDA
and we get our new and improved purchase price.

I knew that this would not be well received by
our buyer and counseled our client accordingly. He
instructed me to raise our price. The good news is
that we had a very good relationship with the buyer
and he did not end discussions. He reminded us
that he had earlier given in to a concession that we

had asked for and we added a couple of other favorable deal points, but he did not move his purchase number.

We huddled with our client and had a serious pros and cons discussion. He did recognize that we had fought hard to improve his transaction. He also recognized that the buyer had drawn his line in the sand and would walk away. The risk that we discussed with our client was that if we returned to market, that would delay his pay day by minimum of 90 days. Also we pointed out that the market does not care why a deal blows up. When you return to the market, the stigma is that some negative surprise happened during due diligence and the new potential buyers will apply that risk discount to their offers.

Our client did agree to do the deal and is very optimistic about the company moving forward with a great partner.

In a post deal debrief with our client I told him that had I to do it again, what I should have said when the buyer requested the delayed closing is, "We know that if you find something negative, you are going to ask for a price adjustment. If we discover something positive will we be able to get a correspondingly positive adjustment. What is he going to say to that?

In reflecting on this situation, I wanted to use my learning to improve our process and I believe that I have come up with the strategy. In our very next deal I incorporated our new strategy. We got several offers with transaction value, cash at close, earnout, seller note and net working capital defined. In our counter proposals we are now proposing the following language:

We propose to pay a multiple of 4.43 times the trailing twelve month (ending in the last full month prior to the month of closing) Adjusted EBITDA, which using full year 2015 Adjusted EBITDA of approximately $1,000,000 results in a valuation of $4,430,000. Adjusted EBITDA for the purposes of this determination will be defined as Net Income plus any One-time professional fees associated with this business sale (currently $42,000 for investment banker fees additional legal and accounting services).

What we are accomplishing with this language is that if the price can go down during the due diligence process, then the price can go up during the process. Why not formalize it because we know that in 99 times out of 100, if the company performance goes down from where it was when the bid was submitted, an adjustment will be applied by the buyer.

If the seller does not relent, the buyer will walk away. The unwritten buyer's rule is that the price can only go down during due diligence. We are out to change that one-sided approach and even the playing field for our sell side clients.

CHAPTER 9

The Value of a Good Advisor

9.1 – New Rules for Merger and Acquisition Success

If you are a business owner considering selling your business, most likely you will interview several business brokers or merger and acquisition advisors. In the process you might hear, "We have lists of qualified buyers." Some potential business sellers find this phrase almost hypnotic. It congers visions of this group of well funded, anxious buyers who can't wait to pay a generous price the moment they are made aware of this great opportunity.

For the larger business owners that are interviewing M&A firms, this "qualified buyers" claim deserves a careful investigation. These M&A firms have lists of hundreds of private equity firms with their buying criteria, business size requirements, minimum revenue and EBITDA levels and industry preferences. All M&A firms have pretty much the same list. There are subscription databases available to anyone. The better M&A firms have refined these lists and entered them into a good contact management system so they are more easily searchable.

The approach these M&A firms with these Private Equity lists employ is to blast an email profile to their list and if they get an immediate and robust response, they will focus on the deal and work the deal. What happens to the 90% of sale transactions that clearly do not fit either the minimum EBITDA and revenue requirements or the conservative valuations of this group of buyers?

Those deals requiring contact with strategic industry buyers usually go into dormant status. They will not be actively worked, but will occasionally be presented in another email campaign, mail campaign or at a private equity deal mart (industry meeting where many M&A firms present their clients to several PEG's).

For the business owner that has paid a substantial up front engagement fee or healthy monthly fees, this is not what you had in mind. The way to get a business sold is to reach the strategic industry buyers. That is not easy. Presidents of companies (the buyer decision maker) do not open mail from an unknown party. So, mailings do not work. Let me repeat that. In a merger and acquisition transaction, mailings do not work.

Presidents of companies do everything possible to keep their email addresses confidential, so email blasts on a broad scale are not possible. Telemarketers are not skilled enough to pass through the voice mail and assistant screening gauntlet. If you have ever tried to present an acquisition opportunity to IBM, Microsoft, Google, Hewlett-Packard or Apple, let's just say it would be easier to get into a castle with a moat full of alligators.

The investment bankers from Morgan Stanley or Goldman Sachs can generally get an audience with any major CEO. However, the fees they charge limit their clientele to businesses with north of $1 billion in revenues. So how do $15 million in revenue businesses get sold? You need to locate a boutique M&A firm that will provide a Wall Street style, active selling process at a size appropriate fee structure.

What does this mean? The approach that consistently produces a high percentage of completed transactions is the most labor intensive and costs the most to deliver. It is an old fashioned, IBM, dialing for dollars effort, starting at the presidential level of the targeted strategic buyers. It usually takes ten phone dials and a great deal of finesse to penetrate the gauntlet and get a forty five second credibility opportunity with the right contact.

If you are able to pass that test and establish their interest, you ask them for their email address so you can send them the blind profile (two page business summary without the company identity) and confidentiality agreement. This is a qualifying test. The president will not give you their email address unless they are serious about the company you have described for sale. If the president is not the appropriate contact, his assistant will generally direct you to the correct party. When that happens, we update our contact management database with this information so on the next M&A engagement we go directly to the proper contact.

Our first engagement in an industry requires a great deal of this discovery process. With each subsequent engagement in an industry, we become increasingly efficient and improve our credibility and brand awareness. There is generally an advantage to engaging an M&A firm that has experience in your industry. After several transactions in a niche, we become that more efficient and effective. Our list truly becomes a list of "qualified buyers."

For example, by our fourth engagement in healthcare information technology, we know the specialty of the top 300 players, we know the lead on M&A deals, we know his direct dial number, email address, and most importantly he knows us.

So, on engagement four in XYZ industry, we put together the blind profile and confidentiality agreement. We get our seller client to approve our list of targeted buyer prospects. We generate our daily hot list of the 20 contacts we will call. We either talk with them directly of leave a voice mail asking them to watch their email for our acquisition opportunity. Our open rates and response rates go up by a factor of 10 X with this labor intensive approach.

Having credibility and brand awareness in an industry helps because we ask them in the email to reply back if they are not interested. We can then update their status on this deal and not continue to try to contact them.

When they are interested, they sign and return the confidentiality agreement. We then email them the Confidential Acquisition Memorandum (the Book). We enter a hot list follow-up in 5 business days. If they remain interested, they will generally have a list of questions they send us. We work with our clients to provide a written response and update the memorandum with a fluid FAQ section that is constantly updated with each interested buyer. This saves us and our clients a great deal of time answering questions only one time.

We have incorporated our FAQ list into our marketing process very effectively. Any time we provide a written response to a buyer, we update the book and we update a stand-alone FAQ document. This FAQ document contains all the questions in date order from all of the buyers. Every time we update the list with new questions, we send it out to every buyer that has previously executed the confidentiality agreement.

Here is our not so subtle message to the buyers, "You are not the only buyer involved in this process." The impact is amazing. The buyers behave much better and they move the process forward at a better pace than they normally would.

Once a buyer's questions are answered, we usually arrange a conference call and Web Demo if appropriate. If the buyer remains interested, we then arrange a buyer visit. This is prepared with the seller as we coach him on what questions to expect and what message he needs to convey.

We also carefully orchestrate the rules and regulations of the visit with both buyer and seller including the visit premise so the employees do not get worried or suspicious. It could be a new banking relationship, an insurance company, or a strategic alliance.

If the buyer remains interested, they may ask for some much more detailed information. At a certain point we have to draw the line on information flow and push for a qualified letter of intent, LOI. In general a LOI says that if we carefully examine your books and records in a due diligence process and confirm everything you have told us so far and discover no materially adverse items, we will pay you $xx for your company with these deal terms and this transaction structure.

In return for that, the buyer will usually require a quiet period. That means that for the due diligence period – usually 30 to 60 days, the M&A advisors are precluded from shopping the deal any further to other potential buyers. This is also called a standstill. If the due diligence is completed without major incident, the buyer's team starts preparing the definitive purchase agreement.

Buyers will often try to misbehave during this process and attack the transaction value with each little nit they uncover. Because we have provided ample reminders to the buyer that there are other interested and qualified buyers involved (remember the FAQ's), we generally are able to discourage this costly behavior.

Once the due diligence is completed, the buyer's team starts preparing the definitive purchase agreement. This is quite detailed and restates the deal terms and conditions and surrounds that with pages of reps and warranties. The business people refine and negotiate the business points while the respective legal teams negotiate the legal points. If there is an impasse, the top business person on each side generally attempts to balance the risk reward legal issue with sound business judgment.

We are almost there. A closing date is set and the parties usually convene in the conference room of the buyer's or seller's outside counsel. The stacks of contracts are reviewed one final time by counsel and the signors walk around the table, adding their signatures. The banker is called and the order is given, "wire the funds." Mission accomplished.

As a business seller, you must recognize that a business sale is a very difficult process. The closing ratios for many of the bigger middle market firms is well below 20%. Our feeling is that the more passive mailing campaign, Private Equity email blast, approach is simply a model that no longer works in this busy, information overload world of the large company CEO.

Think about Oracle trying to sell a $500,000 software project to Fortune 500 companies with a mailing. What about IBM selling a large company on a 10-year $150 million data center outsourcing project with an email blast?

This sounds pretty silly when you think of it. Of course they do not do that. They have highly trained, highly compensated, and highly skilled salesmen that call at the highest levels of corporate America and present the strategic case for their complex and expensive offering. These companies are the best at what they do and understand what it takes to maximize their performance. With a business sale, you have the same type of highly complex, strategic, and expensive proposition. What makes you think that your business sale will be accomplished by any other process than a direct sales approach by highly trained M&A professionals calling on the presidents of the buying companies?

9.2 – Bridging the Valuation Gap Between Business Seller and Business Buyer

In a survey that we did with the Business Broker and the Merger and Acquisition profession, 68.9% of respondents felt that their top challenge was dealing with their seller client's valuation expectations. This is the number one reason that, as one national Investment Banking firm estimates only 10% of businesses that are for sale will actually close within 3 years of going to market. That is a 90% failure rate.

As we look to improve the performance of our practice, we looked for ways to judge the valuation expectations and reasonableness of our potential client. An M&A firm that fails to complete the sale of a client, even if they charged an up-front or monthly fees, suffers a financial loss along with their client. Those fees are not enough to cover the amount of work devoted to these projects. We determined that having clients with reasonable value expectations was a key success factor.

We explored a number of options including preparing a mock letter of intent to present to the client after analyzing his business. This mock LOI included not only transaction value, but also the amount of cash at closing, earn outs, seller notes and any other factors we felt would be components of a market buyer offer. If you can believe it, that mock LOI was generally not well received. For example, one client was a service business and had no recurring revenue contracts in place. In other words, their next year's revenues had to be sold and delivered next year. Their assets were their people and their people walked out the door every night.

Our mock LOI included a deal structure that proposed 70% of transaction value would be based on a percentage of the next four years of revenue performance as an earn out payment. Our client was adamant that this structure would be a non-starter. Fast forward 9 months and 30 buyers that had signed Confidentiality Agreements and reviewed the Memorandum withdrew from the buying process. It was only after that level of market feedback was he willing to consider the message of the market.

We decided to eliminate this approach because the effect was to put us sideways with our client early in the M&A process. The clients viewed our attempted dose of reality as not being on their side. No one likes to hear that you have an ugly baby. We found the reaction from our clients almost that pronounced.

We tried probing into our clients' rationale for their valuation expectations and we would hear such comments as, "This is how much we need in order to retire and maintain our lifestyle," or, "I heard that Acme Consulting sold for 1 X revenues," or, "We invested $3 million in developing this product, so we should get at least $4.5 million."

My unspoken reaction to these comments is that the market doesn't care what you need to retire. It doesn't care how much you invested in the product. The market does care about valuation multiples, but timing, company characteristics and circumstances are all unique and different. When our client brings us an example of IBM bought XYZ Software Company for 2 X revenues so we should get 2X revenues. It is simply not appropriate to draw a conclusion about your value when compared to an IBM acquired company. You have revenues of $6 million and they had $300 million in revenue, were in business for 28 years, had 2,000 installed customers, were cash flowing $85 million annually and are a recognized brand name. Larger companies carry a valuation premium compared to small companies.

When I say my unspoken reaction, please refer to my success with the mock LOI discussed earlier. So now we are on to Plan C in how to deal with this valuation gap between our seller clients and the buyers that we present. Plan C turned out to be a bust also. Our clients did not respond very favorable when in response to their statement of value expectations we asked, "Are you kidding me?" or "What are you smoking?"

This issue becomes even more difficult when the business is heavily based on intellectual property such as a software or information technology firm. There is much broader interpretation by the market than for more traditional bricks and mortar firms. With the asset based businesses we can present comparables that provide us and our clients a range of possibilities. If a business is to sell outside of the usual parameters, there must be some compelling value creator like a coveted customer list, proprietary intellectual property, unusual profitability, rapid growth, significant barriers to entry, or something that is not easily duplicated.

For an information technology, computer technology, or healthcare company, comparables are helpful and are appropriate for gift and estate valuations, key man insurance, and for a starting point for a company sale. However, because the market often values these kinds of companies very generously in a competitive bid process, we recommend just that when trying to determine value in a company sale. The value is significantly impacted by the professional M&A process. In these companies where there can be broad interpretation of its value by the market it is essential to conduct the right process to unlock all of the value.

So you might be thinking, how do we handle value expectations in these technology based company situations? Now we are on to Plan D and I must admit it is a big improvement over Plan C (are you kidding)? The good news is that Plan D has the highest success rate. The bad news is that Plan D is the most difficult. We have determined that we as M&A professionals are not the right authority on our client's value, the market is.

After years of what are some of the most emotionally charged events in a business owner's life, we have determined that we must earn our credibility to fully gain his trust. If the client feels like his broker or investment banker is just trying to get him to accept the first deal so that the representative can earn his success fee, there will be no trust and probably no deal.

If the client sees his representatives bring multiple, qualified buyers to the table, present the opportunity intelligently and strategically, fight for value creation, and provide buyer feedback, that process creates credibility and trust. The client may not be totally satisfied with the value the market is communicating, but he should be totally satisfied that we have brought him the market. If we can get to that point, the likelihood of a completed transaction increases dramatically.

The client is now faced with a very difficult decision and a test of reasonableness. Can he interpret the market feedback, balance that against the potential disappointment resulting from his preconceived value expectations and complete a transaction?

9.3 – How is the Business Selling Price Determined?

Business valuations are a valuable tool to set a range of prices when you sell a business. The only true way to determine value, however, is to present the business to the universe of buyers in a true open market bidding process.

How much are you expecting when you sell your business? I always ask this question of our clients. The answers are as different as the businesses. "We need $5 million to give us the type of retirement we want. We have invested $2 million in the product. Our investors have put in $3 million so far. It should sell for $5 million. I heard that XYZ Company got $30 million for their company." Well, my response to my clients doesn't necessarily endear me to them, but it is the truth. The market doesn't care. The market doesn't care how much it cost you to develop the product or how much your investors have in or how much you need to retire or how much you think it is worth.

The market looks at what the ROI is for its investment in a company. If you are fortunate enough to have a technology that can be leveraged, the market may look at the future returns of that technology in stronger hands.

For most businesses, there are benchmarks that are often used as a starting point. The most common in a merger and acquisition situation is an

EBITDA multiple. That is the gold standard for privately held companies, similar to what a PE multiple is as a business valuation metric for publicly traded stocks. One of the measures that has come into vogue on Wall Street is a PEG multiple or Price Earnings Growth. It is essentially a way to attempt to quantify the difference in PE multiples between two firms in the same industry that have a much different future growth scenario.

A very interesting discovery that we have made in engagements to sell a company that is privately held is that buyers attempt to ignore this factor when making their purchase offers.

We recently represented a company in an M&A deal that was in an industry characterized by slow growth of about 4%, had commodity type products and consequently very thin gross margins, and had little pricing power. Our client introduced a new product that was unique, had very healthy margins, retained some pricing power, and was experiencing 50% year over year growth.

The industry benchmark valuations were at 4.5 X EBITDA. We had the three largest players in the industry all interested in the acquisition and each one put out an initial bid that was, surprise, about 4.5 X EBITDA. Another factor was that our client was in rapid growth mode so a good deal of their costs were front end loaded as they launched a few big box retailers during this period. The effect of this was to depress their EBITDA performance. This made these offers even more inadequate.

The result is that we have a classic valuation gap between business buyer and business seller. This is the biggest reason that many merger and acquisition transactions do not happen. Our clients are terribly disappointed and suggest that these buyers "just don't get it." Our buyers have experience in making several acquisitions in their space and have their business valuation metrics pretty much in stone and think our sellers are being unreasonable in their expectations. Game over, right?

Not so fast. One of the most important roles of a business broker, merger and acquisition advisor or investment banker is devise a transaction value and structure that works for both parties. We go to the buyers and point out that their traditional way of looking at these transactions is appropriate for their prior acquisitions with standard growth metrics, lack of pricing power, and commodity type products. We go to our business sellers and point out that as a small company with a few big box retailers comprising 80% of company sales with essentially one main product, that they have a great deal of small company risk. For example, if the retail buyer from XYZ Big Box Retailer changes and is replaced by a buyer that has a consolidation of vendors bias, then they could lose 30% of their business with one decision. A bigger company, however, with 30 SKU's would be much harder to replace with a change in buyers.

We have established a platform with both buyer and seller to consider alternatives to their hard and fast valuation positions. Here is an example of a business sale transaction structure that could be a win for both buyer and seller:

1. $1,000,000 Cash at Close which is approximately a 4 X EBITDA multiple for the year 2007.

2. An Earn out (Additional Transaction Value) based on SELLER COMPANY'S Sales Revenue beginning in year 1 and ending at the end of year 5. The earnout is at risk, but is set to net the shareholders a 6 X EBITDA multiple on 2008 projected sales (sales $6 million and EBITDA margin of 16.67% or EBITDA of $1,000,000).

This is the transaction structure we are recommending to balance a low EBITDA valuation on a company that will grow revenues by 50% next year. If they don't, then the earn out will be less. Most of the transaction value is in future performance based earn out. Our projection is that with BUYER COMPANY cost efficiencies, BUYER COMPANY can improve operating performance by an amount that covers the entire earn out amount and maintains or even improves SELLER COMPANY'S historical margins.

Most business buyers that approach a company with an unsolicited interest in acquiring them are bottom feeders and will attempt to buy way below the market. They will attempt to draw out the process and pursue several acquisitions simultaneously hoping that one or two sellers just cave and sell out at a discount. They may start out at a decent valuation, but as they go through their due diligence process will find one issue after another that makes them reduce their offer. They often throw out the term "material adverse change" in an attempt to justify their value reducing behaviors. Some business development directors get judged or paid bonuses on how much below the original offer they can ultimately close the deal.

What is the way to combat this bad buyer

behavior? The best way is to have options. Those options are multiple interested buyers. We feel very uncomfortable when we are engaged to sell a company that is difficult to sell. We have taken them through the entire marketing phase and end up with only one legitimate interested buyer. You bet that buyer recognizes the issues and the likelihood of limited interest and will attempt all of the maneuvers to drive down the buying price and terms. Our negotiating position on behalf of our seller client is severely weakened and we struggle to preserve value in spite of doing this every day. Think about how effective you will be in this single buyer scenario. We tell our prospective clients that contact us after an unsolicited offer, "When it comes to business valuation, if you have only one buyer, he is right."

9.4 – How to Increase the Selling Price of Your Business by 40% or More

This sounds like a bold claim, but over our 17 year history in Mergers and Acquisitions we have seen huge swings in value for business sellers that embraced these value enhancing approaches.

Never - Engage with a single buyer who approaches you with an unsolicited offer. This buyer is trying to buy your company at a bargain price. You are either for sale with the full universe of strategic buyers competing for your company, or you are not for sale. This is the number one error business sellers make.

<u>Turn as much of your revenue as possible into contractually recurring revenue.</u> This is exactly why most major software companies are moving away from a one-time licensing fee to a software as a service (SaaS) offering. The time and materials IT service model is disappearing and being replaced with a managed services offering. Contractually recurring revenue tremendously reduces the risk for a business buyer and they will pay up for it both in purchase price and the percentage of cash at closing versus earnouts and deferred contingent payments.

<u>Create and leverage intellectual capital. Just ask a song writer or an author.</u> Disney is a master at creating compelling movie characters and then using them on everything from lunch boxes and underwear to action figures and amusement park rides. For intellectual capital including software, inventions, approved drugs, the labor plus materials metrics of a typical manufacturer do not apply and the gross margins can approach 100%.

Become a voice of authority in your industry.
Be the go-to resource for reporters to comment on industry developments. Blog, write articles, and speak at industry events. Many M&A deals that result in huge premiums for the selling company are the result of also acquiring the company's talent. Take Wal-Mart's acquisition of Jet. How much of that premium price was a result of the visionary CEO Marc Lore and his potential impact on the giant acquiring company. Acquisitions by Google, Facebook, Microsoft and many others feature this premium price for companies with coveted talent.

Understand and document how a large acquiring company could create "strategic value" as the new owner of your company. Capture that in a growth plan document and be ready to articulate that in discussions with potential buyers.

Own your financial statements. When a buyer asks a question on aspects of your financial statements, it is not your accountant's job. It is your job to understand where every dollar comes from and where every dollar goes. The message is that you are in control. If you are wishy washy in this area, the buyer loses confidence in all other facets of your business and will apply their own discount on the entire transaction value.

Diversify your customer base. If you have a major portion of your company's revenues concentrated in a hand full of customers, count on the buyer applying a punishing discount to transaction value and the amount of transaction value you receive at closing. The implied message is that after you leave, your customers will no longer be loyal to the old company. They will hedge their bets with your transaction value.

Do not attempt to sell your company yourself. Here are just a few reasons. You already have more than a full time job. Selling a business is a full time job. Normally a business seller will sell only one business in a lifetime. Experienced buyers have acquired dozens of companies. Their experience will move money from your pockets to their pockets at every stage of the sale process. You will have a very difficult time creating a true soft auction competitive bidding process and will default to processing each buyer in a serial fashion. You lose all competitive leverage. By selling your own business, you alert the world that you are for sale. Your employees, clients, suppliers, and bankers get nervous while your competitors get predatory.

Hire a good M&A advisor, preferably with experience in your industry or market niche to represent you. They will speak the language, so important in establishing credibility with the buyers. They will have a fully developed database with the appropriate M&A contacts at the target buying companies. They will articulate your story to the best buyers. They will balance the experience scales in negotiating price, terms and conditions of your transaction and perhaps more importantly, will defend that value through term sheets, due diligence, contractual negotiations and closing. Finally, they will artfully stimulate the animal spirits of a competitive market to maximize your selling price and terms.

The sad part about business owners who elect to sell their business themselves, is that the only one who knows about the huge haircut they took was the single buyer who is celebrating their bargain purchase.

CHAPTER 10

Getting Across the
Finish Line

10.1 – The Importance of Reasonableness When Selling Your Business

We recently completed a survey of a broad cross section of business brokers and merger and acquisition professionals. One of the questions we posed was, "What is the biggest challenge you face in your practice?" We gave them eight choices including lack of financing, sell side deal flow, not enough buyers, etc. We asked our professionals to pick their top three. The top answer was

Seller Value Expectations with a 68.9% response rate. The next closest answer was sell side deal flow at 55.3%. Why is this the biggest challenge that our industry faces? To me this translates into a great deal of wasted effort on the part of our buyers, our seller clients, and our profession.

This is further exacerbated by the business sellers that expect a full business sale engagement with no monthly fees and the only payment in the form of a contingent success fee. A true professional M&A engagement includes preparation of blind profiles, confidentiality agreements, memorandum authoring, preparing a database of buyers, buyer contact, conference calls, buyer visits and negotiations. A typical business sale takes between 4-12 months and often involves from 500-1,000 hours of Investment Banker work.

Because deal flow is the second largest problem that the industry faces, many business brokers and merger and acquisition professionals will agree to this success fee only seller demand. I believe it was Rockefeller that said, "If it seems too good to be true, it probably is." One of the large industry players estimates that the average business sale closing ratio is less than 10%. This is so important that I am going to say it again. The business sale closing ratio is less than 10%. It fails 90% of the time.

Let's look at the natural result of this dynamic. The business broker, if he is doing it the right way, is going through this very labor intensive process to contact buyers, get confidentiality agreements signed and bring qualified buyers to the table. Here is what typically happens. The owner is getting all of this work for free, has unreasonable value expectations and since he is not paying any fees, has no sense of urgency. The broker could bring in legitimate market offers that are fair and the owner says, "That is not nearly enough, you are doing fine, just keep going."

Well it doesn't take a business broker too many situations like this before something has to change. The first thing that usually changes is that he now refuses to take on any engagements without an upfront payment or a monthly consulting fee to offset some of his costs in this low closing environment. What happens over the next year is that his deal flow totally dries up, because he is competing with those professionals that are still willing to operate with only a contingent success fee.

The next question is how do those brokers that

operate on a contingency basis stay in business? The simple answer is that they can no longer afford to perform a true M&A process. They take on a large number of clients and try to sell their business through newspaper ads, industry publication ads, email blasts to private equity groups, email blasts to other brokers and the favorite – putting the business on several business for sale Web Sites.

All of these approaches, with the exception of contacting private equity firms (about 1 % of businesses for sale meet their rigorous buying criteria) invite individual buyers, not corporate buyers. Individual buyers are looking to buy a job and to the extent that business sellers have inflated value expectations, these buyers have equally deflated valuation expectations. It looks something like this. Do you have the $XXX minimum needed for the cash at closing? No but I have investors. These investors never show up.

The individual's analysis follows this logic. Well, at the height of my career, I was making $150,000, so I am going to have to get at least that out of the business each year. Also, because this is high risk, the equity I put in will command a 25% return, and I have to cover the 75% of transaction value debt at

10%. So, by my calculation I can afford a price of 60% of the true market value of the business.

This gap is almost never bridged between business seller and individual buyer. And yet the approach most of the business broker profession is forced to take based on the unreasonable expectations of the sellers invites this dynamic. This is often hugely damaging to the seller's business. No matter how much he tries to focus on running his business, this stream of bargain hunters is a big drain. The business often suffers a significant drop in performance during this period, and like an overpriced home, often becomes stale in the process.

As the owner of a Main Street Business - bar, restaurant, salon, convenience store, gas station, etc. the economics and the likely universe of buyers really dictate this approach. Just be prepared for this process and at least have your non-paid broker screen out the totally unqualified buyers.

For owners of B2B type businesses and larger businesses, your buyer will not be an individual, but rather a corporation or a private equity group. Let's focus here on the corporate buyer. If the potential buyer is under $50 - $100 million in revenue, the M&A contact is usually the president. If the company is larger, it usually will have the initial deal vetting completed by the head of strategy, business development or mergers and acquisitions. Those people are not visiting business for sale Web Sites or searching the business opportunities section of the newspaper.

The business owner's first reasonableness hurdle is whether he/she recognizes that to reach these corporate buyers is a very difficult and labor intensive process and a firm that specializes in reaching these targeted buyers is the right choice to hire. These professionals normally require either an up-front fee or a monthly fee in addition to the contingent success fee.

Well, you did it. You interviewed several firms, checked references, felt comfortable with their process and felt confident with them as you partner for the next 6-9 months. Your M&A firm takes you to the market and gets several companies interested. You arrange multiple conference calls and corporate visits and then the subject of value comes into focus. This is where deals usually break down. There is a natural valuation gap between buyer and seller and the challenge becomes how to bridge that gap with both valuation and deal structure. The seller's reasonableness will be put to the test as he tries to balance his emotions with the ultimate arbiter of value, the marketplace. But that is the subject of a future article.

10.2 – The Price and Terms of a Business Sale The Offer Depends on the Many Characteristics

We try to prepare our business sellers for the multitude of different deal structures that they should expect from various buyers. We go through elements like cash at close, seller notes, earn outs, non-competes, escrow accounts, etc. More often than not our first time seller will actually put out his or her hand in a stop gesture and reply, "I only want the full price in cash at close." Here we will discuss some of the selling company characteristics that directly affect both the selling price and the terms.

Selling Company Revenue Composition – This is a very important factor in determining how much a buyer will pay for your business and how much will be in cash at closing. If 80% of your annual revenue is a result of contractually recurring revenue, you can command both a premium price and a deal heavily weighted in cash at close. On the other hand, if you have little or no contractually recurring revenue and are heavily dependent on net new sales from new clients, your sale price will be far less and you will be expected to receive a significant portion based on a future performance earn out. Companies that can demonstrate historically repeatable revenue with long term clients will fall between the two extremes mentioned above.

Selling Company Management Depth – If every aspect of the company's business funnels through the two key partners who are close to retirement age and there is a huge gap in management depth and capabilities, this is risky to buyers. They are not inclined to write a big check to the owners only to have them walk out the door with their relationships and knowledge six months later. The more decentralized the customer and supplier relationships are and the more widely dispersed the intellectual property is, the higher the sale price and the higher the percentage of transaction value is at close. If it is all concentrated, the buyer will want the insurance of a transaction structure that pays over time based on future company performance.

Selling Company Customer Concentration –

You can absolutely correlate purchase price and cash at close to this element. Let's say, for discussion purposes, that you had two identical companies in revenues, profits, profit margins, and EBITDA. Company A has no more than 5% of their revenue coming from a single customer. Company B has 40% of its revenues coming from four large blue chip accounts. Company A will sell for a 15-25% premium to Company B. Also Company B will command only 60 to 70 % of the cash at close that Company A commands. Customer Concentration is a big risk factor for a buyer that cannot assume that the relationship dynamics will be the same once the principals leave.

Main Street versus B2B Company - Typically the issue of seller notes comes up with an individual buyer that has limited resources and is attempting to buy a main street type business with as much leverage as possible. Corporate buyers seldom utilize this vehicle.

Escrow Account Requirement – This is a portion of the purchase that is held by a third party Escrow Agent with instructions on how the funds can be released to the seller. These are typically required by a buyer where they perceive the risk of a future event such as product liability, a pollution issue, or an outstanding law suit. The funds are held for a period that could extend for several years if there are unresolved issues of this nature.

Professional Services type firm – Your company literally walks out the front door each evening. These may be consulting firms, accounting firms, executive recruiting firms, ad agencies, etc. Your producers have developed their book of business and their loyal account relationships. Your clients are customers of the company, but may be more loyal customers of their professional contact person. Sales transactions for this type of firm can involve a very heavy earn out component to protect the buyer from a mass exodus of clients because the professionals leave the firm post acquisition and take their clients with them.

Non Compete Agreements – these are pretty much standard for prudent buyers buying a company and not wanting to defend themselves against the former owner who gets bored with retirement and decides to start a similar business. The seller should get some compensation for the agreement and the more restrictive the agreement, the higher the compensation.

Stock Sale versus Asset Sale – Most large corporations "have a policy" that they will only do asset acquisitions as opposed to buying the stock of a target company. There are some very good reasons to do this. When you do a stock purchase you get all the assets and all the liabilities both known and unknown. If you look at the reasons buyers have escrow accounts, many of the same reasons apply for wanting to do an asset acquisition. They simply are buying identified assets and the remaining corporate shell is still owned by the previous owner with all the liabilities not specifically identified in the asset purchase agreement.

If the seller is a C-Corp, however, it is a major negative from a tax perspective to do an asset sale because the sale of assets is taxed as ordinary income at the corporate tax rate. The proceeds are taxed again at the owner's long term capital gain rate when the funds are distributed to him. For companies that do not have the escrow type potential liabilities, a stock sale may work. A buyer could successfully offer a significantly lower price with a stock purchase than a competitor requiring an asset purchase. The seller should analyze the two transactions from an after tax proceeds perspective to determine the superior offer.

If you are a business owner contemplating a business sale and you want the highest purchase price and the most cash at close, analyze your company based on the factors above. If you can implement changes that correct some of these risk factors you improve your odds of your best exit.

10.3 – While Selling Your Business - Steady as She Goes

When we first engage with a new client, we sit down with them and give them the talk. No, not the birds and the bees talk, but the talk about what they should and should not be doing while the sale process is going forward.

Our first bit of advice is to keep your eye on the ball. It sounds simple, but the business sale process is disruptive. The smaller the company with fewer management personnel, the more disruptive. We tell our clients to maintain their focus on running the business and rely on their mergers and acquisitions advisors to manage the business sale process. That being said, there are many demands placed on the owners for answering buyers' questions, conference calls, corporate visits, evaluating buyers and their offers, and negotiating.

If the disruptions cause the sales and profits of the business to fall, the buyer does not care that they fell because the owners were distracted. They only care about the bottom line performance of the business. The sale process generally runs for a period of eight months to over a year in many cases. The original financials in the offering memorandum are often supplemented several times as each quarter passes. If you have received purchase offers based on one set of financials and those financials deteriorate, you can count on the offers being lowered across the board to reflect your company's new reality. If the downturn is sizable, it may interfere with the buyer's ability to secure financing, especially if the buyer is a private equity group.

Many owners want to juice their sales while the business is being sold to drive every last bit of value into their business sale price. They want to bring on that extra salesman or launch that big marketing campaign in order to spike their sales and profits and then get rewarded with a 5 X EBITDA bump in the business selling price. This is very expensive flawed logic on the part of the business owner. A new salesman, even an outstanding new salesman is a drain on the company profitability for 9 months to a year. That is the best case scenario. In the majority of cases the new salesman does not make the grade and is fired. His loss, however, hits the company's financials.

A marketing campaign is not always the sales driving engine the owner hopes it will be. But, for discussion sake, let's say that the campaign was well conceived and executed. The full impact of the campaign is usually delayed by six months to a year. If this occurs during the business sale process, the financials reflect the drop and the lowering of the buyers' offers will follow as surely as the next sunrise.

The cruel irony of this dynamic is that you are investing to make the business more valuable for you to sell, but instead are giving the buyers an opportunity to buy at a discount. Your investment then pays off a year after the new owner has taken over.

OK, I admit, I have painted the worst case scenario. So let's say that the salesman you hired was a real star or your marketing campaign caused sales and profits to spike in the near term. You, the business seller, now with the upper hand, go back to your buyers with a business selling price increase commensurate with the buyer reductions sited above. The reaction you get from the buyers is not at all what you expected, however. Instead of raising their offers by your increase in EBITDA multiplied by your prior offer valuation metric, they refer to this increase as an anomaly or an outlier. Instead of rewarding you proportionately in the purchase price, they want to normalize this over the prior three years.

For clarification, let's look at the following example. Your 2011 EBITDA was $2,000,000, 2012 was $2,200,000 and 2013 was $2,400,000. You are selling your business starting in June of 2014 and you launch your successful marketing campaign that boosts your EBITDA to $3,200,000 in 2014. Your offer on the table was 5 X 2013 EBITDA or $12,000,000. You go to your buyer and say my new price is 5 X 2014 EBITDA or $16,000,000. The buyer (especially if they are a Private Equity Group or financial buyer) will say, wait just a minute, this was an anomaly and we need to normalize that over the past 4 years. So they add up all of the EBITDA numbers and divide by 4 to get a normalized EBIT-DA of $2.45 million. They raise their purchase offer from $12,000,000 to $12,250,000.

So you have taken on a large financial risk to invest in your business to increase your sales and profits. You beat the odds in achieving a short term bump and your buyers attempt to minimize the impact on their offer price.

On the other side of the ledger, some owners attempt to significantly cut costs during the business sales process. We advise against this approach as well. If the market does not provide the selling price that the owners are satisfied with, they will simply not sell. If you have temporarily slashed your Research and Development or Training budget for the sale, those cuts could come back to hurt you, should you not sell your business near term.

The lesson here is steady as she goes while you are in the midst of your business selling process. A fall in profit is punished and an increase is not rewarded in proportion to the investment or the risk.

10.4 – Some Thoughts on Seller Earnouts

Contrary to what many sellers believe, an earn out component to a business sale is not necessarily a bad thing. As an M&A firm, we see the incidents of bad buyer behavior, but if properly used an earn out can be an excellent tool to maximize seller proceeds. First rule of earn outs – if you do not trust the buyer, there is not enough contractual language available to protect you. I will go one further. If you do not trust the buyer, do not do any kind of deal with him.

If you are negotiating the sale of your business, you want an earn out to be structured so that if the guy you negotiated with and was the deal champion gets "hit by a truck" his replacement cannot interpret the agreement to your detriment. If you can, you want to have your earn out based on top line sales as opposed to division profits, for example. It is amazing how an overhead allocation from corporate can wipe out your division's earnings.

So once you have your earn out based on top line revenue are you safe? What if your company's product were added to the acquirer's suite or products? What if your product were used as a loss leader to help sell the other products? Just like that, your earn out revenue disappears. The way to protect yourself is to establish a minimum sales price for your product for purposes of your earn out calculation. You don't want to try to dictate pricing to the new owner. You simply want to be given fair credit for the revenues that would have resulted had your product sold at historical levels.

In spite of the risks, however, there are many reasons a seller would want to employ an earn out to maximize his business valuation. Here are a few:

1. The seller has several big deals in the sales pipeline and wants to get paid for them. The buyer is going to heavily discount those forecasted deals if he is backed into an all cash at close structure. If the seller is willing to share the risk for those deals closing with an earn out component tied to the deals, the buyer will be much more generous. If the deals don't close, it costs the buyer nothing. If they do close, he is happy to write you the earn out check.

2. The seller anticipates that product sales will explode once the buying company integrates it with their distribution network. If the seller does not have strong sales or profits, but has a great product, it will be difficult to get the optimal selling price using historical sales and profit figures. Rather than take a low price based on those numbers, it may be better to bet on future performance and base a major component of transaction value on sales generated by the much larger company. Receiving 20% of a 10 times greater sales number as an earn out is a big win for the seller.

3. An earn out can help bridge the value gap

between buyer and seller and be the needed catalyst to getting the deal completed.

The use of an earn out can be appropriate as a way for a seller to maximize his sales proceeds in the right circumstances. Just remember that the buyer champion that has established a relationship with you and is compelled to honor the intent of the earn out agreement will most likely be transferred or promoted before your earn out term is completed. You now are in the position of having this agreement interpreted by a person who has no connection or loyalty or knowledge of the intent or the agreement. His mode will be to interpret the agreement in a way to "minimize the expense of the future payment." Just make sure that interpretation cannot destroy the economics of the deal you originally negotiated.

10.5 – Why Earnouts Make Sense Today

The purpose of this section is to present earnouts to sellers of technology companies as a method to maximize their transaction proceeds. Sellers have historically viewed earnouts with suspicion as a way for buyers to get control of their companies cheaply. Earnouts are a variable pricing mechanism designed to tie final sale price to future performance of the acquired entity and are tied to measurable economic milestones such as revenues, gross profit, net income and EBITDA. An intelligently structured earnout not only can facilitate the closing of a deal, but can be a win for both buyer and seller. Below are ten reasons earnouts should be considered as part of your selling transaction structure.

1. Buyers acquisition multiples are at pre 1992 levels. Strategic corporate buyers, private equity groups, and venture capital firms got burned on valuations. Between 1995 and 2001 the premiums paid by corporate buyers in 61% of transactions were greater than the economic gains. In other words, the buyer suffered from dilution. During the 2008 - 2013 period, multiples paid by financial buyers were almost equal to strategic buyers multiples. This is not a favorable pricing environment for tech companies looking for strategic pricing.

2. Based on the bubble, there is a great deal of investor skepticism. They no longer take for granted integration synergies and are weary about cultural clashes, unexpected costs, logistical problems and when their investment becomes accretive. If the seller is willing to take on some of that risk in the

form of an earnout based on integrated performance, he will be offered a more attractive package (only if realistic targets are set and met).

3. Many tech companies are struggling and valuing them based on income will produce some pretty unspectacular results. A buyer will be far more willing to look at an acquisition candidate using strategic multiples if the seller is willing to take on a portion of the post closing performance risk. The key stakeholders of the seller have an incentive to stay on to make their earnout come to fruition, a situation all buyers desire.

4. An old business professor once asked, "What would you rather have, all of a grape or part of a watermelon?" The spirit of the entrepreneur causes many tech company owners to go it alone. The odds are against them achieving critical mass with current resources. They could grow organically and become a grape or they could integrate with a strategic acquirer and achieve their current distribution times 100 or 1000. Six % of this new revenue stream will far surpass 100% of the old one.

5. How many of you have heard of the thrill of victory and the agony of defeat of stock purchases at dizzying multiples? It went something like this –

Public Company A with a stock price of $50 per share buys Private Company B for a 15 x EBITDA multiple in an all stock deal with a one-year restriction on sale of the stock. Lets say that the resultant sales proceeds were 160,000 shares totaling $8 million in value. Company A's stock goes on a steady decline and by the time you can sell, the price is $2.50. Now the effective sale price of your company becomes $400,000. Your 15 x EBITDA multiple evaporated to a multiple of less than one. Compare that result to $5 million cash at close and an earnout that totals $5 million over the next 3 years if revenue targets for your division are met. Your minimum guaranteed multiple is 9.38 x with an upside of 18.75x.

6. Strategic corporate buyers are reluctant to use their devalued stock as the currency of choice for acquisitions. Their preferred currency is cash. By agreeing to an earnout, you give the buyer's cash more velocity (ability to make more acquisitions with their cash) and therefore become a more attractive candidate with the ability to ask for greater compensation in the future.

7. The market is starting to turn positive which reawakens sellers' dreams of bubble type multiples.

The buyers are looking back to the historical norm or pre-bubble pricing. The seller believes that this market deserves a premium and the buyers have raised their standards thus hindering negotiations. An earnout is a way to break this impasse. The seller moves the total selling price up. The buyer stays within their guidelines while potentially paying for the earnout premium with dollars that are the result of additional earnings from the new acquisition.

8. The improving market provides both the seller and the buyer growth leverage. When negotiating the earnout component, buyers will be very generous in future compensation if the acquired company exceeds their projections. Projections that look very aggressive for the seller with their pre-merger resources, suddenly become quite attainable as part of a new company entering a period of growth. An example might look like this: Oracle acquires a small software Company B that has developed Oracle conversion and integration software tools. Last year Company B had sales of $8 million and EBITDA of $1 million. Company B had grown by 20% per year. The purchase transaction was structured to provide Company B $8 million of Oracle stock and $2 million cash at close plus an earnout that would

pay Company B a % of $1 million a year for the next 3 years based on their achieving a 30% compound growth rate in sales. If Company B hit sales of $10.4, $13.52, and $17.58 million respectively for the next 3 years, they would collect another $3 million in transaction value. The seller now expands his client base from 200 to 100,000 installed accounts and his sales force from 4 to 5,000. Those targets should be very easy to hit. Lets assume that through synergies, the buyer improves net margins to 20% of sales and the acquisition produces $2.08, $2.70, and $3.52 million of additional profits respectively. They easily finance the earnout with extra profit.

9. The window of opportunity in the technology area opens and closes very quickly. An earnout structure can allow both the buyer and seller to benefit. If the smaller company has developed a winning technology, they usually have a short period of time to establish a lead in the market. If they are addressing a compelling technology gap, the odds are that companies both large and small are developing their own solution simultaneously. The seller wants to develop the potential of the product to put up sales numbers to drive up the company's selling price. They do not have the distribution channels,

the resources, or time to compete with a larger company with a similar solution looking to establish the industry standard. A larger acquiring company recognizes this first mover advantage and is willing to pay a buy versus build premium to reduce their time to market. The seller wants a large premium while the buyer is not willing to pay full value for projections with stock and cash at close. The solution: an earnout for the seller that handsomely rewards him for meeting those projections. He gets the resources and distribution capability of the buyer so the product can reach standard setting critical mass before another large company can knock it off. The buyer gets to market quicker and achieves first mover advantage while incurring only a portion of the risk of new product development and introduction.

10. You never can forget about taxes. Earnouts provide a vehicle to defer and reduce the seller's tax liability. Be sure to discuss your potential deal structure and tax consequences with your advisors before final negotiations begin. A properly structured earnout could save you significant tax dollars.

Smaller technology companies have many characteristics that make them good candidates for earnouts in sale transactions: 1. High growth rates

2. Earnings not supportive of maximum valuations 3. Limited window of opportunity to achieve meaningful market penetration 4. Buyers less willing to pay for future potential entirely at the sale closing 5. A valuation expectation far greater than those supported by the buyers. It really comes down to how confident the seller is in the performance of his company in the post sale environment. If the earnout targets are reasonably attainable and the earnout compensates him for the at risk portion of transaction value, a seller can significantly improve the likelihood of a sale closing and the transaction value.

10.6 – Deal Structure And Taxes

Do not under estimate the importance of the tax impact in the sale of your business. As an M&A intermediary and member of the IBBA, International Business Brokers Association, we recognize our responsibility to recommend that our clients use attorneys and tax accountants for independent advice on transactions.

As a general rule, buyers of businesses have already completed several transactions. They have a process and are surrounded by a team of experienced mergers and acquisitions professionals. Sellers on the other hand, sell a business only one time. Their "team" consists of their outside counsel who does general business law and their accountant who does their books and tax filings. It is important to note that the seller's team may have little or no experience in a business sale transaction.

Another general rule is that a deal structure that favors a buyer from the tax perspective normally is detrimental to the seller's tax situation and vice versa. For example, in allocating the purchase price in an asset sale, the buyer wants the fastest write-off possible. From a tax standpoint he would want to allocate as much of the transaction value to a consulting contract for the seller and equipment with a short depreciation period. A consulting contract is taxed to the seller as earned income, generally the highest possible tax rate. The difference between the depreciated tax basis of equipment and the amount of the purchase price allocated is taxed to the seller at the seller's ordinary income tax rate. This is generally the second highest tax rate (no FICA due on this vs. earned income). The seller would prefer to have more of the purchase price allocated to goodwill, personal goodwill, and going concern value. The seller would be taxed at the more favorable individual capital gains rates for gains in these categories. An individual that was in the 40% income tax bracket would pay capital gains at a 20% rate. Note: an asset sale of a business will normally put a seller into the highest income tax bracket.

The buyer's write-off period for goodwill, personal goodwill, and going concern value is fifteen years. This is far less desirable than the one or two years of expense "write-off" for a consulting agreement.

Another very important issue for tax purposes is whether the sale is a stock sale or an asset sale. Buyers generally prefer asset sales and sellers generally prefer stock sales. In an asset sale the buyer gets to take a step-up in basis for machinery and equipment. Let's say that the seller's depreciated value for the machinery and equipment were $600,000. FMV and purchase price allocation were $1.25 million. Under a stock sale the buyer inherits the historical depreciation structure for write-off. In an asset sale the buyer establishes the $1.25 million (stepped up value) as his basis for depreciation and gets the advantage of bigger write-offs for tax purposes.

The seller prefers a stock sale because the entire gain is taxed at the more favorable long-term capital gains rate. For an asset sale a portion of the gains will be taxed at the less favorable income tax rates. In the example above, the seller's tax liability for the machinery and equipment gain in an asset sale would be 40% of the $625,000 gain or $250,000. In a stock sale the tax liability for the same gain associated with the machinery and equipment is 20% of $625,000, or $125,000.

The form of the seller's organization, for example C Corp, S Corp, or LLC are important to consider in a business sale. In a C Corp vs. an S Corp and LLC, the gains are subject to double taxation. In a C Corp sale the gain from the sale of assets is taxed at the corporate income tax rate. The remaining proceeds are distributed to the shareholders and the difference between the liquidation proceeds and the stockholder stock basis are taxed at the individual's long-term capital gains rate. The gains have been taxed twice reducing the individual's after-tax proceeds. An S Corp or LLC sale results in gains being taxed only once using the tax profile of the individual stockholder.

<u>Selling your business – tax consideration checklist:</u>

1. Get good tax and legal counsel when you

establish the initial form of your business – C Corp, S Corp, or LLC etc.

2. If you establish a C Corp, retain ownership of all appreciating assets outside of the corporation (land and buildings, patents, trademarks, franchise rights). Note: in a C Corp sale, there are no long-term capital gains tax rates only income tax rates. Long-term capital gains can only offset long-term capital losses. Personal assets sales can have favorable long-term capital gains treatment and you avoid double taxation for these assets with big gains.

3. Look first at the economics of the sales transaction and secondly at the tax structure.

4. Make sure your professional support team has deal making experience.

5. Before you take your business to the market, work with your professionals to understand your tax characteristics and how various deal structures will impact the after-tax sale proceeds

6. Before you complete your sales transaction work with a financial planning or tax planning professional to determine if there are strategies you can employ to defer or eliminate the payment of taxes.

7. Recognize that as a general rule your desire to "cash out" and receive all proceeds from your sale immediately will increase your tax liability.

8. Get your professionals involved early and keep them involved in analyzing various bids to determine your best offer.

Again, the purpose of this article was not to offer you tax advice (which I am not qualified to do). It was to alert you to the huge potential impact that the deal structure and taxes can have on the economics of your sales transaction and the importance of involving the right legal and tax professionals.

10.7 – The Eleventh Hour Deal Change

The next line could be, "Will it Derail Your Sale?" We have seen it go both ways, unfortunately.

If a deal does blow up, everybody loses. The seller has spent six months of divided focus and many of the normal business development activities have been put on the back burner. His or her business will simply not be as strong if the business sale process is not completed.

Normally a buyer that has made it to this point is the one that recognizes the most strategic value and has indicated their willingness to pay for that value. The second, third, and fourth place buyers, if they even have been uncovered, are generally far short of the winning bidder. We have had some very specialized companies that were great fits for only one buyer and the next best bid was less than 50% of the leader's offer. That is not a very attractive backup plan, should the best buyer go away.

The buyer is also damaged by an eleventh hour deal blow up. They have devoted senior level people to analyzing, negotiating, preparing for the integration of the two companies, etc. It often involves several hundred thousand dollars of opportunity costs. If the target company was the answer to a gap in the buyer's product set, they will no longer be able to recognize the anticipated benefits unless they now build it themselves or go acquire the next best target company. Both of these approaches are expensive and time consuming.

Let's get back to the root of the problem. What would cause a buyer to make an eleventh hour change? Our experience has shown that in 80% or more of the cases, it has been the buyer's corporate counsel or outside counsel. They have discovered a deal component that when memorialized in a definitive purchase agreement is either not legal or violates the corporate "risk versus reward covenant."

This is where it gets emotional. It is done "after we had a deal.' We coach our sellers up front and warn them that this can happen. The way we position it is that as a simple matter of logistics, the buyer's legal team has very limited detailed involvement prior to crafting the definitive purchase agreement. In the heat of negotiations, however, the M&A guys have often agreed to something that will not pass the protectors of the mother ship (corporate counsel). When the particular deal term moves the Risk/Reward needle into the red zone, the corporate counsel over rules the M&A guys. An example of this would be an earn out that was open ended and not capped - simply unacceptable on Wall Street.

Another manifestation of the eleventh hour change is the buyer's business development team is tasked with bring the deal along to a point with final approval reserved for the president or the board. Sometimes the M&A team simply commits to something that gets rejected in the final approval process. Unfortunately, sometimes this is real and sometimes it is a popular negotiating ploy called deferring to the higher authority. It can be very tricky determining which is real and which is negotiating.

O.K. So we have established that more often than not, the seller will encounter the dreaded eleventh hour deal change. How should he or she respond?

First Rule - be prepared and know that it is part of the normal process. Do not put it into the category of this is the evil empire looking to beat up the little guy.

Second Rule - Do not destroy your personal good will with the buyer. Often times, the owner has huge value to the buyer in terms of post acquisition product integration and education on their market. If this last minute deal change turns you into Mr. Hyde at the negotiating table, the buyer's Risk/Reward needle could be moved into the red zone. If they view you as someone that could damage company morale or who will be high maintenance or worse, will be litigious, they will walk away from the deal at this point.

Rule Three - If you feel you are about to explode in front of the buyers, ask for a 15 minute break, go into another room and unload on your advisors. Get it out of your system, calm down, and go back into problem solving mode.

Rule Four - Let your advisors do your bidding. Recognize that this is an emotionally charged area for you and it is essential for you to preserve your relationship with your future employer. Let your M&A advisor or your attorney be the bull dog, not you.

Rule Five - Respond in kind at the appropriate economic level. Do not look for a pound of flesh to compensate you for your sense of moral indignation. In corporate America it's not going to happen. Work with your advisors to identify the extent of the economic value you have lost due to the change. Ask for concessions in return that match the economics of the buyer's change.

Rule Six - Keep your eye on the prize. In this very emotional time, you must prepare yourself to be an economic being. If your next best buyer is $2 million below your current buyer's offer, do not put the deal in jeopardy by violating Rules One through Five for a change with maximum impact of $20,000. Put your ego on the shelf, step back, keep your moral indignation in check and preserve your good will. Remain fluid and creative while allowing your advisors to take on the role of the bad guy. Get your deal signed, enjoy your new substantial bank balance, and prosper as a prized member of your new company.

10.8 – Business Sale Negotiation - Our Most Unusual Deal Term

The deal process is very stressful so every once in a while it is refreshing when we can break the tension with a good laugh. In retelling this story I am changing the names to honor the privacy of our clients and buyers. So let me set the stage. We have negotiated and have received a dual signed letter of intent between our client, a privately held healthcare information technology company and a much larger publicly traded company. We are ending due diligence and have had some very stressful discussions regarding the future role , title, salary and duties of our founder/seller. We were able to come to agreement and had started the process of crafting the definitive purchase agreement. So the basic economics of the deal are set, but just need to be memorialized in a formal contract.

I get a call from our client, let's call her Sarah. She says that she is going to fax me over a document and after I read it, to call her back. A minute later the fax starts to print out a page from the buyer's annual report where they identify the price and terms of another acquisition they had completed during the reporting period. I recognized the company because Sarah and I had discussed it before and she had shared that the company was similar to hers in terms of product offering and revenues. In my mind I had formulated a potential transaction range for this very similar company.

We had been able to negotiate what we felt was a very favorable deal for our client, well beyond a typical EBITDA financial buyer valuation. Because it had strategic value to a couple of the major players in the space and we had them both competing for the acquisition, we were being valued at a multiple of revenue not a multiple of EBITDA.

Back to the fax. I start reading the deal terms being described about this very similar company and the valuation was significantly above our lucrative offer. I call up Sarah and the first thing she says to me is, "I want Becky's deal." Becky was the owner of the other acquired company and she and Sarah were professionally acquainted. Being the cool-headed deal guy that I am, I stammered, "Sarah, I looked at this deal and there is no way I can justify the price that the buyer paid for them." She said to me, "Didn't I tell you that Becky was having an affair with the buying company's previous CEO?"

OK now is my time to actually be cool-headed. I said, "Well Sarah, are you prepared to come up with that deliverable, and how will your husband feel about that deal term?" Silence followed for what seemed like an eternity. Soon the silence was broken with a very loud and hearty belly laugh from the other end of the phone. Finally she said, "OK, OK, I get it. Let's get my deal done."

Whew, I dodged a bullet there and even got a funny story out of it. It was not funny until the substantial wire transfer had hit Sarah's bank account.

Made in the USA
Middletown, DE
24 February 2018